"Our clairvoyance is the cornerstone of our spiritual perspective. When we activate and develop this spiritual ability, we allow ourselves to take charge of our lives and our creativity."

BOOKS BY MARY ELLEN FLORA

The *Key Series*:

> **Meditation**: Key to Spiritual Awakening
> **Healing**: Key to Spiritual Balance
> **Clairvoyance**: Key to Spiritual Perspective
> **Chakras**: Key to Spiritual Opening

It is recommended that you read the *Key Series* in the order indicated above. Each book acts as a spiritual textbook to provide a foundation in basic spiritual techniques which helps you prepare, on a level of spiritual awareness, for the next book. All of the material is of a spiritual nature. Allow a spiritual perspective and you will benefit from the information. You must practice the techniques for them to work for you because you cannot intellectualize spiritual information.

The *Energy Series*:

> **Cosmic Energy**: The Creative Power
> **Earth Energy**: The Spiritual Frontier
> **Male and Female Energies**: The Balancing Act
> **Kundalini Energy**: The Flame of Life

CLAIRVOYANCE

Key to Spiritual Perspective

Second Edition

by Mary Ellen Flora

CDM Publications   Everett, Washington

Requests for such permission should be addressed to:

> CDM Publications
> 2402 Summit Avenue
> Everett, WA 98201

First Edition 1992.
Second Edition 2001.

Library of Congress Cataloging-in-Publication Data

Flora, Mary Ellen.
    Clairvoyance : key to spiritual perspective / Mary Ellen Flora.--2nd ed.
        p. cm.
    Includes index.
    ISBN 1-886983-13-5 (pbk. : alk. paper)
     1. Clairvoyance. I. Title.

BF1325 .F57 2001
133.8'4--dc21

                                                  2001025092

Printed on recycled paper in the United States of America.
Malloy Lithographing Inc., Ann Arbor, Michigan

THIS BOOK IS
DEDICATED TO
M. F. "DOC" SLUSHER
FOR HIS NEUTRALITY AND
USE OF GOLD ENERGY.

ACKNOWLEDGEMENTS

Many thanks to all who have helped with the second expanded edition of this book. Special thanks to Carrie Harris for her excellent graphic art for the cover and diagrams. Thank you to Jeff Gibson and Johanna Stark for their artwork.

I greatly appreciate the work and support of Melissa Carmichael as our production leader. Many thanks to Kim Zirbes for her physical and spiritual support. Special thanks to Stacy Rice for leading the publications team and constantly encouraging everyone, including me.

Lembi Kongas has been a support in this book as in previous ones, and her editing and proofreading skills are a gift to the whole team. Thanks also goes to Sara Canady and Patrick Bartmess for their proofreading. Much appreciation goes to Jeff Rice for his work on the index.

Continued appreciation to those who helped produce the first book, which is the foundation of this edition, especially Bill Broomall, Alison Eckels, Jeff Gibson, Gail Coupal, and Reggie Taschereau.

Most of all, I wish to express my love and gratitude to M. F. "Doc" Slusher who has taught me to be strong enough to follow my path.

TABLE OF CONTENTS

INTRODUCTION

To use clairvoyance is to reflect light. When we reflect the light of God within, we see clearly. This ability to reflect light and see clearly is one of the greatest gifts from God to humankind. With clairvoyance, we can see through the darkness we have created in our world and see ourselves and each other as spirit.

Clairvoyance simply means clear seeing. It is the ability to see clearly as spirit. In order to utilize this ability to the fullest, you have to realize that you are spirit. However, many people use their clairvoyance without being aware of using it. For example, successful business people use their clairvoyance to "read" people and situations and to make clear decisions. Most would call this ability intuition, or business sense, or another intellectual term, rather than acknowledging it as their clairvoyance.

Everyone is clairvoyant, but not everyone acknowledges and uses this ability. Most people have been invalidated about their clairvoyance. The negation of this spiritual ability is caused mainly by people's fear of being seen. When we can overcome the fear of seeing clearly and of being seen, we discover a great joy. We discover the joy of spiritual awareness and communication.

For many years, I have helped people activate and use their clairvoyance. Another obstacle that most people have to overcome, in addition to their fear, is their doubt, which comes from the intellect. Since childhood, they have been told that this spiritual ability is not real, so they have to clear the invalidation and doubt which are created by the negation. They have been taught to use the intellect instead of clairvoyance. Ideally, we can use both our intellect and our clairvoyance.

I have been aware of and have used my clairvoyance since childhood, and my family and friends believed that I was strange because of it. They were especially upset when I refused to give up seeing nonphysical things as I grew up. I believe they hoped this "seeing the unseen" was something that I would outgrow.

I remember one incident that frightened my mother and sister as I had seen something they knew I could not be aware of physically. The incident concerned the death of my horse, Ginger, who was a beloved friend for over ten years. The horse had died while at my uncle's farm, and my aunt called to inform my mother. My mother and older sister knew how fond of the horse I was, so they were concerned about how I would feel. They carefully began to explain what had happened, but before they could,

I interrupted them and told them I knew that Ginger had died. They were shocked by my awareness because there was no physical way I could have received this information. I then told them that Ginger was fine, she had enjoyed her life, and I did not feel upset because I knew my friend was with God.

This and other experiences surprised my family, but eventually they came to accept this type of incident, if not to appreciate it. However, many families do not accept the spiritual awareness of children and program them to turn their abilities down or even to turn them off. This is a tragedy of our world because it adds to the already overwhelmingly materialistic view of reality and eliminates the spiritual perspective.

Many people are angry about the invalidation they experienced as children when they communicated spiritual information and were told that it was not real. We all receive programming that the only thing which is real is that which we can touch with our hands, see with our eyes, or in some way experience with our physical senses. This makes us, as spirit, feel like prisoners in our bodies and physical world. It keeps us from seeing what is going on spiritually. Spiritual blindness makes us feel helpless to create what we need in order to accomplish our spiritual goals.

If a family does allow a child to have his clairvoyance, the family usually encourages or even forces the child to give up talking about what he sees when he goes to school. If the family does not program the individual to stop "seeing," then the peer group usually does. The peer group is another powerful force that stops communication about clairvoyance. The group wants physical proof because they have been taught by their adult role models to require it.

We do not have to learn to be clairvoyant. We do have to clear the barriers to our clairvoyance which we have been given and which we have accepted. Spiritual students go through a period of frustration when they begin to open clairvoyantly because they want immediately to see clearly. They have to go through a process of clearing the old programming and other barriers before they can see as clearly as they wish. A time of cleansing is necessary to bring the vibration in the body back up to a level where clairvoyance can be fully experienced.

One student struggled with his clarity for several months. He came to me one day and asked for help, and together we found the issue stopping his clear seeing. I asked him what he did not want to see. He began to cry as he looked at the pain from his childhood which he had wanted to avoid. He spent several months clearing the pain he had let himself see. From then on, his clairvoyance improved and his enthusiasm for clairvoyant reading increased a great deal. The important lesson he learned is that if you wish to see others clearly, you must first see yourself clearly.

Another student had a different problem. She was young and enthusiastic. Her clarity was remarkable. She could see auras, mental image pictures, guides and other spiritual phenomena without any difficulty. Her problem was that she could not talk about the information. She could barely talk to most people about what she saw. When she did communicate, she invariably invalidated the information almost as she said it. With personal meditation, she uncovered the criticism she had received as a child because she saw reality differently from those around her. When she recognized and released the criticism, she could express her views more clearly. Another lesson for her was to be patient with herself and accept that life experience would bring her a greater ability to communicate the wealth of information she saw.

When we allow ourselves to talk about what we see clairvoyantly, we find many others who also acknowledge and use this skill. We open the door to spiritual communication, and it enhances our neutral perspective of life. By using our clairvoyance in communication, in healing, in our creative projects and in accomplishing our life goals, we create a clear spiritual view. If we use only our physical senses, it is like walking under water, feeling heavy and unable to function fully. We can walk above the water when we use our clairvoyance. We can use our spiritual view to stay above the emotional and other physical pulls. Walking on water can represent staying above the emotions and desires of the body, and clairvoyance helps us see how to do this.

Many people who see spiritually keep quiet about it because they believe they are strange or crazy, and they do not want to be ostracized. Some people who come to me are afraid they are insane. They describe seeing things such as colors, lights, ghosts, angels, and other nonphysical phenomena. It is a pleasure to be able to inform them that they are not crazy; they are clairvoyant. We can all see vibrations in the form of color, beings without bodies, and other spiritual phenomena when we open our awareness to the spiritual realm.

Unfortunately, our spiritual abilities have often been associated with insanity. This does not encourage anyone to talk about their clairvoyant experiences. It is time we begin to speak of our spiritual abilities with reverence instead of fear. One man I know asked me fearfully if he was crazy because of a beautiful communication he had with his spiritual guides. When he realized he had nothing to fear, he opened up and communicated many of his other spiritual experiences. He is now using his spiritual communication to heal himself instead of stopping the healing with his fear.

One important aspect of clairvoyance is the neutrality it provides. Neutrality allows us to see and accept things as they are. It is the ability to see without judging.

This aspect of clairvoyance has brought many people a great deal of joy. One student had left his home when he was quite young and made his way on his own. By the time I met him, he had become very judgemental about his family. As he developed his clairvoyance, he began to see his family differently. He also became much more accepting of himself. Eventually he saw how he was blaming himself for his father's death, and his guilt was keeping him in fear and hate. He forgave himself and the rest of his family, and they were reunited after fifteen years of separation. His clear seeing helped him through his pain back to those he loved.

Another man was separated from his mother when he was a small child. The pain from this separation created many problems for him. He had problems with his own son and dark moods he could not explain. When he developed his clairvoyance, he was able to see the painful experiences from his childhood. This helped him accept his mother and forgive her. He is now planning to see her after twenty years of silence.

A woman I know was distraught about her inability to get along with her daughter. She finally gave up trying to heal the relationship and focused on healing herself. As she healed, she opened clairvoyantly and saw that she had been invading her daughter's personal space all of their life together. At first she would not accept what she saw. She eventually developed her amusement enough to forgive herself. She is still learning not to be so invasive, but has pulled back into herself enough that her daughter will relate to her now.

A personal lesson in refocusing on clairvoyance and non-judgement occurred when my husband had a heart attack while we were on vacation in Mexico. This was a very disturbing experience for me, mainly because I was afraid of losing my best friend. In addition, we were away from familiar surroundings and the support of friends and family.

The first twenty-four hours, I was immersed in the physical demands of emergency details. After that intense period, I had a great deal of time to focus on the situation. My first thoughts were judgemental. I judged myself and my husband for allowing such a thing to happen. Then I judged myself more for judging my husband, since he was ill. Then I judged him for being ill. I had a fine time wallowing in judgement for a few hours.

Fortunately, I regained my spiritual perspective rapidly. I realized we had each created this experience for our learning and each of us had a different lesson from the same circumstances. When I saw clearly what my lesson was and took responsibility for myself, I gave my husband permission to do the same. As he told me while I was in the midst of my turmoil, "Mary Ellen, you can't solve my problems."

When I viewed the experience as spirit, I could accept each of us as we were, learning and growing. We were two capable beings using our bodies to learn and progress. I even managed to forgive us for being human and allowed amusement into the situation. My lessons were learning not to judge how we create in order to learn, and to accept things as they are, without taking responsibility for anyone except myself. We can change anything within ourselves when we see it and accept it as it is instead of fighting it.

Using clairvoyance is an important step in acknowledging ourselves as spirit. Our clairvoyance is the cornerstone of our spiritual perspective. When we activate and develop this spiritual ability, we allow ourselves to take charge of our lives and our creativity. Our clairvoyance is a spiritual ability to be used in our communication, healing and creativity.

The techniques and encouragement that follow can help you either to begin using your clairvoyance or to continue to use it with greater clarity and certainty. It is time for all of us to wake up, see who we are and see where we are going. We are spirit. We are returning our attention to God.

*"Clairvoyance
makes life infinitely
more interesting
because it opens your
awareness to the total
picture and helps keep
you from being focused
on the surface or on
one part of the scene."*

CLAIRVOYANCE

Everyone is spirit. Everyone is a part of God. Clairvoyance is a gift from God to help us see our way in this physical world. We have great need of our clairvoyance since we have put so much of our energy into the physical world. We have become so enthralled with the world, we allow ourselves to be entrapped by it. Our clairvoyance can help us find our way back to our spirituality and out of the physical web. It reflects light in the darkness. With clairvoyance, we can see the spiritual way through the physical maze. We can see ourselves as spirit and a part of God. Continuing to shine the light of clairvoyance, we can discover our spiritual path which is our way to God.

Clairvoyance simply means *clear seeing*. It is the ability we all have as spirit to see clearly. Information about our clairvoyance is located in the brow chakra, also known as the sixth chakra. Chakras are energy centers which contain spiritual information. The sixth chakra is associated with the pineal gland. Scientists have recently acknowledged this gland as a reflector of light. The spiritual purpose of the sixth chakra is to reflect the light of God within us.

Clairvoyance allows us to see things of a spiritual nature, such as vibrations that manifest as color in the auras of all living things. We can also see spirits that do not have bodies. We can see the pictures, symbols and formulas that each soul uses to communicate. Clairvoyance enables us to open to the spiritual world and bring it into our physical consciousness and our life.

With our clairvoyance, we have a clearer perception of this and all realities. We are not limited to the physical perception because we can see the spiritual realm as well. When we see clearly, we make decisions with all available information, rather than using only part of it. Clairvoyance can be used in every aspect of life, both spiritual and physical.

This spiritual perspective allows us the awareness that we are spirit and that all things are of a spiritual nature. It also helps us to see our path in life and how best to solve our problems and accomplish our goals. Without our clairvoyance, we are spiritually blind and feel as if we are helpless and groping through life. When we, as spirit, focus into the sixth chakra and awaken our clairvoyance, we turn on the light of spirit in our lives.

The use of our clairvoyance develops neutrality. Seeing from a spiritual perspective gives a full view and thus a neutral view. When we are neutral, we can accept things the way they are. It is like seeing the view from the top of the hill instead of from the bottom or from halfway up the hill. We have a full perspective that enables us to see the total picture when we view life from the sixth chakra. With this view, we can make clearer decisions because we have more information. Neutrality comes from this clear, full perspective since we can see what is and are not limited by what we or others wish us to see. We can then accept what is and not pretend that things are as we wish. This neutral view moves us above the emotional level of the body. We can easily get caught in confusion when we are overwhelmed by the body's emotions.

Clear seeing allows us not to judge ourselves and others. When we have the total picture, we can see other people's creativity as well as our own more clearly. We may be judging someone because he is creating pain in our life. When we move into a neutral space, we can see that the person is only sharing what he has within himself. With this clairvoyant perspective, we can attempt to help the other person to clear his pain, without having to judge him. Without judgement to cloud our vision, we can see if we need to move away from this person so he no longer affects us. Forgiveness allows us to let go of another person; judgement will hold someone to us. The use of clairvoyance helps us cleanse judgement and create forgiveness.

Forgiving ourselves and others allows us to be spiritually free.

Unfortunately, judgement is second nature to us all. We are brought up with judgement. Some religions and groups teach that judgement is beneficial. We are taught that there is right and wrong about everything. We are taught our society's brand of good and bad. Depending on the sector of society in which you were brought up, you were taught that rich is good and poor is bad, or vice versa. The list of things we are taught to judge is endless. Some people are taught to judge one religion and some are taught to judge another. Many people are taught to judge a racial group or two. Most are taught that one gender is better than the other.

Society teaches us to judge from our birth onward. Our family, school, religious training and the rest of society teach us to judge. We learn what is good and bad from advertising and other forms of media. Judgement has become part of being in a body. It is one way the body controls its reality, as judgement is based on physical phenomena. As spirit, we are here to overcome this limitation of the body, this judgement. It is an interference to seeing ourselves and others as spirit. It focuses our attention on some aspect of body reality, such as the color of the skin, the gender of the body or the amount of possessions. All of these characteristics relate to survival issues intead of spiritual creativity.

We need unique circumstances to learn and grow since each of us is here for a unique learning experience. When we judge ourselves or others, we deny this uniqueness. Any time we judge another person, we are also judging ourselves. When we judge, we are not allowing others their unique experience in life. When we do not allow others their experience, we do not create space to have our personal learning experience.

If we judge someone who is of a different religion from ourselves as wrong or misguided, we are not allowing ourselves to operate as spirit. We are not using our clairvoyance, or clear seeing, and allowing the other person her chosen path. We judge her as wrong and ourselves as right. This limits both parties involved by not acknowledging that each lesson is correct for the individual creating it. Judgement is a body survival technique that interferes with a spiritual perspective.

Healing occurs when we accept ourselves and others as we are and move above the survival pull of the body. By eliminating judgement and criticism, we allow growth and change. We cannot change or heal without first accepting things as they are. Spiritual freedom is possible when we recognize things as they are, not as we wish them to be. It is not necessary to agree with the other person to accept him where he is. We do not even need to like what he is doing in order to see him and accept him without judgement.

You can dislike something and still allow yourself to be neutral about the situation when you use your clairvoyance and simply see what is. You can even disagree with someone without judging her for her views or actions. Your clairvoyance helps you do this because you see yourself and others as spirit, not just as bodies. For example, you may not like or agree with your sister's political beliefs, but you can allow her to have her views without changing your own beliefs.

Judgement stops communication. As spirit, our greatest love is communication, so judgement invalidates us as spirit and veils our love. Non-judgement means accepting things as they are, seeing that we are growing and progressing through our life lessons and temptations as planned. If we make a mistake or do not create what we like, we can change our situation once we accept it as it is. When we do not like another, we can change that by changing our perception and releasing the judgement we have of the other person. We can learn not to believe our survival is dependent on judgement.

The concept of tolerance is an appealing one because it means freedom from prejudice and allows us to accept the world's amazing variety. Instead of wanting things the way we believe they should be and judging them when they are not, we can practice tolerance, allowing things to be as they are. Everything is unique, and there is no standard or ideal. Tolerance allows freedom, while judgement brings us slavery.

When we realize the value of clairvoyance in creating our life on earth with tolerance, we can commit ourselves to opening and developing this God-given ability. When we do this, our communication and creativity take on new meaning and dimensions. Our clairvoyance enhances our ability to love.

For example, if you view a disagreement with a friend strictly from a physical perspective, you will believe that one of you must be right and one of you must be wrong. When you allow your clear seeing, you will see both sides of the issue. You will see what you and your friend are attempting to learn and what you need to heal in yourself to change the situation. By using your clairvoyance, you can see yourself and your friend as spirit. Both of you can gain a great deal by learning the lessons for which you created the disagreement. If nothing else, you will see whether the disagreement is important or not.

Clairvoyance makes life infinitely more interesting because it opens your awareness to the total picture and helps keep you from being focused only on the surface or on one part of the scene. Looking at the world without your clairvoyance is like trying to watch a stage play while sitting behind a post. You cannot see most of the scenes and have to guess at the action taking place. You can become fixated on one actor or one part of the play and miss the main theme of the presentation. Clairvoyance opens your view to the whole stage and brings this world to life because you can see all of the action, both spiritual and physical.

Clairvoyance is a vital tool in healing. When we want to change something or heal it, we need to see all that is happening so we know what to do. With the spiritual perspective, we can see if the issue is a spiritual or a physical one. We can then decide what is needed for a healing to take place. If we do not use our clairvoyance in healing, we will see only the physical issues and will keep repeating the problem. Many healers define their clairvoyance as intuition, the art of healing, or something else. In reality, when someone is a good diagnostician, he is using his clairvoyance.

By using your clairvoyance, you can see what needs to be healed within yourself. When you see this, you can make the necessary changes for healing to occur. If you see that your hate is making your body sick, you can cleanse the hate from your system and eliminate the illness. Or you may see that the stress in your work is causing you to have difficulties in your home life and can make the necessary changes to create the balance needed for healing.

Or you could use your clairvoyance to see that the pain in your arm is a past pain experience that has been stimulated and that you can use meditation to cleanse the area. The list goes on and on with ways you can use your clairvoyance to see the way to heal yourself.

There are many purposes for clairvoyance in this world. We need it to make decisions, to forgive ourselves and others, to heal, and to see what we are creating and how our creations are affecting ourselves and others. We need our clairvoyance to see ourselves and others as spirit so we can practice tolerance and learn to be loving.

The spiritual perspective provided by using our clairvoyance opens new vistas of spiritual awareness. When we see what is occurring, instead of what others want us to see, we are in control of our lives. We can follow our unique path instead of one that someone else wants us to follow. For example, a parent may want a child to follow a certain profession, and the child may not want to because it is not his path. If the child allows the parent to cloud his decisions and choices into adulthood, he will not see what is correct for him to accomplish his life goals. Without this clarity, a soul could misuse an entire life cycle. Clairvoyance helps one to see what is his own and what belongs to someone else. My husband went to the University of Washington Dental School. He told me that he met several students who were in dental school because their dads were dentists, not because they wanted to be dentists. This is true of many professions. My husband said the drop-outs were those who did not have a strong desire to follow that difficult path. Hopefully, those students found their unique paths. My mother wanted me to be a teacher because she was a teacher. I did not want to teach school and was strong-willed enough to find my unique avenue of teaching. Of course, my family called me stubborn instead of strong-willed. Clear sight helped me see my path.

There is a great deal of confusion about clairvoyance. Some of this comes from misinterpreting this ability. Many believe it is for telling the future, reading people's minds, or playing parlor tricks. While you can use your clairvoyance along with other spiritual abilities to do these things, they are not the meaning or purpose of clairvoyance.

Clairvoyance is our ability to see clearly as spirit. It is our spiritual sight. When we use it, we can see spiritual reality. When we do not use it, we are blind to the spiritual realm within and around us. We need to give up our fear of our spiritual abilities, including clairvoyance, and begin to use them in a mature manner.

God gave us clairvoyance to allow us to see as spirit so that we could make our decisions from this mature level and not from the limited level of the physical perspective.

The purpose of our clairvoyance is to see our way to focus on God. If we are blind, we will not see our way and will remain lost in the physical world. When we activate our clairvoyance, our path becomes clear and easy to follow.

Clairvoyance does not negate any religious beliefs or groups since there are many paths to God. It allows the individual to see her personal path clearly and to follow it with joy. Since our path may not be the same one as our parents' or friends', we need to see what is correct for us and to allow our friends and family to pursue the spiritual path which is correct for them. Clairvoyance enhances our relationship with God and with all the great teachers and prophets because we can see their message and see how to live it more fully. Clairvoyance increases our awareness of God and enhances our relationship and communication with all things.

With our clairvoyance, we can see many things in life that we may have been blind to before. We can see why we chose our parents, siblings, mates and children as our partners in learning for this life. We can see when we are acting on our own and when we are being manipulated by others. We can see when we are manipulating others. We gain our personal power and clarity as we see what is and cease to be fooled by the illusion of the physical veil.

We can use our clairvoyance to validate reincarnation or the experience of living in many different bodies over time. This validation of reincarnation helps us to understand ourselves as spirit and our creativity and learning process. Reincarnation is simply a way for us to learn lessons through time. Our clairvoyance helps us take advantage of the past lessons by seeing the past information in the present to help us continue our growth and complete cycles.

We can better understand our present life by using our clairvoyance to read past lives and see the previous relationships we had with others. We can see if we are operating from this past information instead of the present circumstances. If a relationship with a parent is always difficult, we could be trying to solve problems brought forward from a previous lifetime. When we see the past life and complete the cycle, we can interact in present time.

A young friend of mine was in love with her father and jealous of her mother's relationship with him. This caused conflict in the family. She came to me for a clairvoyant reading, and I saw several past lives when she and her father had been husband and wife or lovers. She changed her perspective of her relationship with her parents as soon as she had this information. She started to relate to them in present time with their present roles. The family was able to interact more comfortably after that.

We can see past lives clairvoyantly without having to regress into them to re-experience them. We can gain clarity about the previous life lessons without the trauma of reliving the past. Regression validates the existence of reincarnation but is not necessary to gain the information and healing we are seeking. With clairvoyance, we can see clearly and create the change without reliving the experience. Several students of mine tried regression in their spiritual search before they discovered their clairvoyance. Most of them found the experience of reliving past lives traumatic. They all said using their clairvoyance to see the past was more controlled and less disturbing than re-experiencing the past.

Reincarnation is one way we learn spiritual lessons through time. We take different bodies in various situations to learn what we need to know. We may take a male body to learn about aggression or a female body to learn about being receptive. We may take a body that is not physically whole to learn a lesson about humility or about healing on a spiritual level, instead of strictly by the physical rules. We choose life experiences in bodies where we are rich and others where we are poor, each offering opportunities to learn about ourselves.

Through reincarnation, we create bodies of a variety of races and cultures to learn the many lessons offered on our Earth. As spirit, we create every manner of experience in order to become the mature beings we wish to be. We have to learn compassion, strength, neutrality and so much more. Most importantly, we have to learn to know ourselves as spirit. Reincarnation allows us to learn our lessons by providing us the time and opportunity to learn and grow. Some beings have to create similar problems or experiences several times to learn a given lesson. The important point is to continue learning and growing in order to progress along our spiritual path.

There are many paths to God, and each path can lead us to our Source. We have experienced moving toward God through many religious structures and spiritual beliefs. Reincarnation is not contradictory to any religious beliefs because it is a part of our spiritual school, just as religions are. Reincarnation provides us with a variety of learning opportunities, including the opportunity to experience God through many different religions.

The fear many have of the belief in reincarnation usually stems from a lack of information. Fear can also come from the threat of being ostracized by a group that denies reincarnation. With the belief that there is only one life, the soul believes he must learn everything at once and has only one chance to return to God. With this belief, a group can easily dictate to the individual soul what it must do to achieve maturity. The group can effectively use guilt and fear in manipulating the individual to its own ends instead of nurturing the soul to help the individual achieve its personal goals. If a soul accepts this belief of one life, it does so because it has something to learn. This and other limiting beliefs are part of our collective consciousness since we have the free will to choose our path. We can choose to be free or enslaved. We can choose to be focused spiritually or physically. Every focus is an opportunity to learn something, and there are an infinite variety of options to meet the needs of each emerging soul.

Our clairvoyance helps us see what is correct for us in any lifetime and helps us use the information we have already gained through previous lives. When we look at ourselves from a neutral, spiritual perspective, we can see the tapestry of learning we have woven for ourselves. We can see what threads are out of place and if any are missing. If we need to, we can repair our tapestry and continue joyfully with the weaving of our unique soul personalities. When the tapestry is complete, we are ready to present ourselves whole to our Creator. Reincarnation allows us to learn, to make mistakes and to correct the mistakes during our creative process. Clairvoyance allows us to see what we are doing so we can move with greater ease along our creative, spiritual path.

Our ability to see clearly helps us see what we wish to keep and what we wish to release as we move along our way. It does not mean we have to put up with things we do not approve of or do not like. It simply means we can understand what is behind the physical action and thus have a clearer perspective of what we wish to do, if anything. Our clairvoyance can help us see that it is best to allow some things to be as they are. Action can be healing, and it can also be interference. When we see, we know whether it is beneficial to act or simply be.

You will find your life changing as you become clearer. You may choose new friends because the ones from your past are not in agreement with seeing and being seen. This can bring you sadness and a sense of loss because your life is changing. It can also bring a feeling of joy because you free yourself from limits placed on you by others. Either way, you often part company with friends and even family when you put your attention on the spiritual way. Not everyone wants to be spiritually aware: you have to allow others their way of life in order to be free to have your own. There are those who wish to stay focused on the physical and do not wish to focus on spirit and God. With your clairvoyance, you can see this and let them be as they are. You can learn to be loving during the transitions that take place in your life.

It can be emotionally painful to let go of those you love who no longer wish to interact with you because you open spiritually. Even your neutral perspective will not eliminate the body's reaction to the separation. Your neutrality does allow you to see that you do not lose any soul. You are simply separated from another on a physical level, not the spiritual level. Since each soul needs to follow his or her own path, these seeming separations are necessary for each to complete his goals. Not everyone wants to be clairvoyant and aware of what is being played out both physically and spiritually. Some prefer to accept the surface appearance and stay focused on the physical play. It is important not to judge either choice because your judgement will block your growth.

The opening of the sixth chakra is a challenging game. You need to be aware of the importance of joy and enthusiasm in your process so your seriousness does not stop your progress. If you are too serious, your lessons become a chore rather than a joy. When you are amused, you learn more rapidly and accomplish your lessons faster. You need to learn both to welcome and to let go of others joyously.

Every other person in our life reflects an aspect of ourselves and offers an opportunity to acknowledge and heal that aspect within ourselves. It is helpful to see others from neutral to know what part they are playing in our learning process. It is also helpful to be in neutral and to allow our amusement when we see things in others that we do not like and realize the same things are in us.

Spiritual opening can be a joyous process. We need to remind ourselves of this joy when we run into difficulties and create pains along the way. The energy level of God is best described in this reality as enthusiasm. When we are enthusiastic, we are close to God and our lessons in this realm become lighter and easier. Being happy and amused helps us be closer to our God.

Misunderstanding and misinformation about clairvoyance can interfere with the joy of using it. Some confusion about clairvoyance comes from its misuse. There are some who have opened this ability and have used it for their self-aggrandizement. When someone uses any spiritual ability for personal gain and power games, she will eventually lose it. As you focus on your clairvoyance, remember this temptation, and stay true to yourself as spirit. Be in touch with your God, and all things are possible for you, including happiness.

Often people use their clairvoyance to focus on the future. This can cause confusion because the power of creation is in the present moment. We can read the past, present and future clairvoyantly, but we gain the greatest power and clarity when we focus in the present as we use our clairvoyance. When we read past lives or have them read by another reader, we can benefit most when we relate them to the present incarnation: what does that past existence mean to us today? When we read the future, we need to remember that all futures are only possible futures and can be changed. Many people want a clairvoyant to read their future because they want to experience the "magic" of spiritual abilities. While the magic is wonderful, we have to be aware that we are the ones responsible for what we create, whether it is in the past, present or future. We may create something because it was predicted even if it is not appropriate when we arrive at that crossroad.

Our concepts of perfection about clairvoyance can also interfere with our use of this ability. When we expect ourselves to see things a certain way, it keeps us from seeing things as they are. Our desire for perfection is a barrier to our spiritual abilities as perfection is a lie. Perfection does not allow for the reality of variety and choice. When we let go of the desire to see perfectly and allow ourselves to see what is there, we can experience the joy of seeing spiritually. Looking clairvoyantly, we see that our desire for perfection is actually competition with God because only God is perfect. We experience perfection only when we return completely to God.

I know a woman who is so devoted to creating her idea of perfection that she is afraid and miserable. She grew up trying to meet her mother's expectations, and instead of rebelling against those unrealistic demands, she adopted them as her own. She cannot succeed at any business venture because her expectations keep her from dealing with things as they are. She cannot be happy because nothing in her life is good enough to meet her expectations. She has created a loving husband and delightful children but cannot enjoy them because they do not meet her expectations.

Another example of how a desire for perfection can interfere with your clairvoyance is trying to see things the way you believe someone else sees them. You may know someone you admire as a clairvoyant and attempt to see things the way they do. This is not possible because you are not the other person. This attempt to meet your perfect ideal will stop your clairvoyant development since you will be trying to be something you are not. Each soul sees things in a unique way.

If you persist in trying to be like your ideal, you will use effort and try very hard to be clairvoyant. This effort will stop you from seeing clearly. Effort is a body energy, not a spiritual energy, and clairvoyance is a spiritual ability, thus physical effort will deflect your spiritual ability. It is natural and necessary to use effort in physical matters. We have been so focused on the physical that we have to train ourselves to let go of effort in order to use our spiritual skills. We cannot use effort with any of our spiritual abilities because it blocks the flow of spiritual energy.

The intellect is another aspect of the body that we have to train ourselves to discipline as we open clairvoyantly. The intellect will constantly try to pull our attention back to the physical realm. It will project doubt and confusion. We have to refocus our attention on our clairvoyance in order to learn how to move above the body's intellect in order to gain a clear perspective of spiritual reality. Since many have been taught that the intellect is the highest attribute attainable, we have to unlearn some childhood programming to move on to the broader realm of spirit. The intellect is extremely beneficial, but not an upper limit of understanding.

If we limit ourselves to the intellectual view, we limit ourselves to the body and physical perspective. The intellect is an aspect of the body and therefore cannot comprehend many aspects of spiritual reality. When we let go of these limits and allow ourselves to see things that are not understood by the intellect, we move into the spiritual realm. That is why faith is so important. We eventually have to rely on our faith to take the leap from the physical to the spiritual perspective. Our faith can help us move from our intellectual view to our clairvoyant view.

We have become so enamored with our intellects that we often forget that there is reality beyond anything we can comprehend in the body. So much credence has been given to the intellect that we often use it as a weapon to try to destroy spiritual awareness, instead of using it to improve our lives. The intellect has also become a favorite defense mechanism. We hold it up to protect ourselves from pain and fear. If we feel intellectually justified, we seem able to allow all kinds of injustice and blindness regarding both ourselves and others.

It is time to move into a more mature state of being in which we can use the intellect and not be limited by it. The intellect can be used to enhance life in the physical world without letting it hold us to a physical perspective. When we tune in to our clairvoyance, we can see spiritually, perceiving the intellect as a tool to be used, not a limit to hold us to the Earth.

In the development of our clairvoyance, we need to be vigilant that we do not put physical rules on this most helpful of abilities. We must remember that we see the world through our own eyes, whether physical or spiritual. Our view of life colors our perspective, and this affects our interpretation of everything we see. When we open clairvoyantly, we have to clear inappropriate concepts so we do not judge or program others. Remaining in touch with ourselves and God as we develop allows us to maintain our spiritual perspective and not get lost in the physical vibration. Self healing, clearing our energy system, is essential to clear development. If we wish to serve, we must first prepare ourselves.

The development of clairvoyance and the sixth chakra does not guarantee a clear view, since it is tied in with the opening of the remainder of the chakra system. It does help us to open clairvoyantly to see the wealth of spiritual information around us and to learn daily how to become clearer with this ability. The sixth chakra is one of the least difficult of the chakras to open safely. The sixth is important in the opening of the other chakras because it gives us a clear, spiritual perspective of our system and our creativity.

Viewing life from the sixth chakra and the clairvoyant perspective can bring great joy and make the journey of spiritual opening well worth the attention. We can see life as a lesson, a journey, a spiritual awakening, rather than a series of problems or futile actions. Our relationship with everyone becomes clearer because we see the spiritual nature of our interactions. What we may have been seeing as an unpleasant encounter may be seen as an opportunity to heal. We begin to see the lessons others are attempting to learn and find ourselves to be more forgiving and more tolerant of others. We no longer judge others' actions as foolish or meaningless, but see them as spiritual lessons.

Clairvoyance can be used to improve all aspects of life. Until everyone regains their clairvoyant abilities, it would help to have skilled clairvoyants in professional capacities to help everyone to see issues more neutrally. Since we can focus our clairvoyant abilities in different ways, some would discover an ability to diagnose disease and could assist the medical profession. It would be a great assistance to a doctor to have an accurate diagnosis from a clairvoyant perspective. Simply knowing whether the disease is physical or spiritual in origin would be of great value, and a clairvoyant could see this easily. The police have already used clairvoyants effectively in solving cases and finding lost persons. When clairvoyance is generally accepted, the police can more easily use skilled clairvoyants for many aspects of their work. Lawyers can use their own clairvoyance or the abilities of a professional to help tell the truth from a lie. A clairvoyant can see when someone lies by seeing if their aura shimmers. This would be helpful in many legal situations.

There are so many practical ways we can use our clairvoyance in everyday life, the list could go on to include everything we do. While many are becoming aware of this ability, they can take advantage of those who have already developed this spiritual skill. Hopefully, everyone will eventually wake up to this spiritual ability so that we can all see again as we were meant to before we lost ourselves in the physical world.

Clairvoyance is a spiritual ability that we all have, one that is well worth the time and attention necessary to open and use it. It allows us to be neutral, non-judgemental, accepting of what is, forgiving and in charge of our life. Clear seeing lets us see ourselves and each other as spirit, a part of God, worthy of respect and reverence. We see who we are and what we are here on this Earth to accomplish.

Clear seeing is necessary for clear living. By living each lifetime clearly, we accomplish our goals and move forward on our spiritual path. When we see all that is happening within and around us, we make clear decisions. This clarity builds confidence that allows us to discover compassion, joy and eventually love within ourselves.

Clairvoyance is a gift given freely, and it is up to us to use it wisely to create a spiritual awareness which will lead us to God. When we see clearly, we are a healing presence to ourselves and the whole world.

*"When you continue
to let yourself see
spiritually, you learn to
accept things as they are
and learn not to be so
affected by what you see.
Then it is possible to
rejoice in the spiritual
validation that comes
from this awareness."*

SPIRITUAL TECHNIQUES

The techniques presented here can assist you to open your clairvoyance in a healing manner. They can help you tune in to yourself as spirit and to your God within. They are meant to assist in your spiritual development. The techniques are: grounding, being in the center of your head and sixth chakra, running earth and cosmic energies, visualization, the aura and telling a truth from a lie.

Opening and developing any of your spiritual abilities requires patience and perseverance. You need to be cautious in your work. If you open carefully and in a healing manner, you will be in charge of the process. If you hurry, force yourself or skip steps, you can disturb your system. You will then have to take time out to heal the damage.

The techniques are intended to help you to see yourself and others from a neutral, non-judgemental perspective. When you see your creativity from the spiritual perspective instead of from the body's view, you are free. You experience freedom from hate, fear, doubt and the other debilitating body energies that hold you in slavery to the material world. You move above the pull of the body's desires and problems for a clearer view of your world.

Opening our clairvoyance, or the ability to use our spiritual sight, is one of our most important developmental steps. We need the information in the sixth chakra to help us avoid the pitfalls of judgement and other limits of a strictly physical perspective. How many have lost faith in God by trying to explain a physical trauma in physical terms only? Without the spiritual perspective provided by the view from the sixth chakra, one can easily get lost in lies and judgement.

An example is a friend who took care of her mother during the end of her mother's life. It was a difficult time because her mother had colon cancer but no one knew it until after exploratory surgery, during which her mother died. The period before the mother's death was confusing and disturbing since she was in pain and distress and the daughter did not know if from real or imagined causes. The daughter was resentful of her mother's needs, demands and problems. She did not have a spiritual view of the situation and spent her time blaming everyone for the inconvenience, expense and disturbance she was caused. She created a rift in communication with her siblings because of her view and disrupted the support she had. A spiritual perspective would have helped her see this time with her mother as an opportunity to heal past pains and misunderstandings. She would also have seen the opportunity to heal herself in ways her mother did not.

One temptation when opening the sixth chakra is to believe that you see everything and therefore know what is best for everyone. This causes an ego problem which will interfere with further development. You must regularly clear your energy system to maintain your neutral, clairvoyant perspective. A different problem can come from seeing only what you want to see, rather than allowing yourself to see what is. You need to relate to this world as it is in order to use your clairvoyance effectively in it.

My friend, who is a capable clairvoyant, saw only what she wanted to see: herself as a martyr who was taken advantage of, her siblings as selfish and uncaring and her mother as crazy and mean. Her perspective was through her beliefs and from a strictly physical view. A clearer spiritual view could have included: herself as a healer who did not heal herself, her siblings giving up seniority to her authority in the family and her mother in fear and pain. Clairvoyance can be used incorrectly if the person is not healing herself and allowing the full picture.

When you first put your attention on your clairvoyance, you may find the experience frightening. Since you are probably programmed to believe that you are just a body and not spirit, you may encounter fear from your body when you first experience the reality that you are spirit.

This fear may originate from your childhood training which tells you that clairvoyance is evil. It can come from seeing things that upset you, or from seeing the unpleasant aspects of life you may have previously avoided. When you open clairvoyantly, you eventually see the total spectrum, both the ugly and the beautiful and everything in between.

When you continue to let yourself see spiritually, you learn to accept things as they are and learn not to be so affected by what you see. Then it is possible to rejoice in the spiritual validation that comes from this awareness. You will gain greater control, through practice and perseverance, as you continue to use this spiritual skill.

Continue putting your attention on your clairvoyance by using the techniques regularly. A daily meditation focusing on your clairvoyance will eventually bring you to the clarity you seek. Use the techniques to keep you on track and your faith to inspire you to keep going.

The techniques are best experienced when you are in a quiet place. Sit in a straight-backed chair with your feet flat on the floor and your hands separated in your lap. Sit with your spine as straight as possible because a straight spine helps your energy move smoothly.

Take a few deep breaths to relax your body and enjoy each technique. After practice, you will easily combine the techniques to create a meditation that can assist you to open your clairvoyance. Enjoy.

GROUNDING

Grounding is a spiritual technique to connect you, the spirit, to your body, and you and your body to the planet. Grounding is essential to the beneficial development of any of your spiritual abilities because it puts you, the spirit, in control of your creativity and anchors you in the present reality.

Grounding is a connection between your first chakra, which is located near the base of your spine, and the center of the Earth. Your first chakra contains your information about how to relate to the physical world. The grounding cord connects you to this physical world. When grounded, you can see more clearly because you are relating to this reality in a controlled manner. You are anchored instead of being afloat.

Your grounding acts much like an electrical ground. You, as spirit, have a great deal more energy than your body. When you, the energetic being, enter your body, your grounding cord enables you to release excess energy. Grounding connects your body to the Earth so it feels safe with all of your spiritual energy.

Grounding is an important foundation when opening your clairvoyance. Your grounding cord connects you to the physical world and allows you to open to the spiritual realm safely. Grounding keeps you in touch with your body and your physical creations while you re-learn to see spiritually. Grounding is the foundation for building your spiritual awareness. Grounding from the first chakra helps you be senior to all things.

The technique of grounding also helps you release energy. You can let go of any energy down your grounding cord. You can release foreign energy, excess energy or energy you no longer want. This ability to release allows you to eliminate the usual build-up of energies in your system that can cause discomfort, disease, tension and other problems.

Grounding enables you to connect and stay in touch with both spiritual and physical realities and to release unwanted energies. When you ground, you have much greater control of all of your abilities and your creativity.

EXPERIENCE your grounding now. Sit in a straight-backed chair with your hands separated in your lap and your feet flat on the floor. Take a few deep breaths to relax your body.

VISUALIZE a cord of energy flowing from your first chakra, located near the base of your spine, to the center of the Earth. Breathe deeply, and allow your body to relax with being grounded.

VISUALIZE THE GROUNDING CORD as a laser beam of energy going from your first chakra to the center of the Earth. Allow the energy to flow freely to create a strong connection.

EXPERIENCE your grounding cord. Be aware of the effect it has on your body. Acknowledge your body's reaction, and work with your body as you ground through it.

ALLOW ANY ENERGY interfering with your grounding to flow down the grounding cord. Let the grounding cord be a release for any excess energy in your body that is making it uncomfortable. Be aware of your grounding as a connection to the Earth and a way to release energy.

AGAIN, BREATHE DEEPLY, and visualize energy flowing from your first chakra to the center of the Earth. Be still, and experience your grounding cord.

The more you use your grounding cord, the more effective it will be for you. You can be grounded at all times. You can be grounded when sitting, standing, walking or in any position. You can use grounding in any circumstance. Experiment with your grounding while standing in line somewhere, while having a conversation or while working. The more you use your grounding, the more it will help you. Always use it in your meditations.

Whenever you are focused on opening or using your clairvoyance, ground yourself. Your grounding will make you and those around you safer and more comfortable. Your grounding assists you to be in control of your physical and spiritual experiences.

Some things you see when you open clairvoyantly can be disturbing. Your grounding is essential to help you deal with the emotional reaction of your body when you become spiritually aware. Being clairvoyant does not eliminate the emotional messages of the body, though it helps you move above the emotions. Grounding is essential because it allows you to be in charge as spirit and to maintain your spiritual perspective. Without grounding, it would be difficult, if not impossible, to maintain a clear view of reality because, without this spiritual connection, the body would pull you back to its perspective.

With grounding, you can constantly change by releasing energy. By being connected to the present physical reality with your grounding, you are stable and secure. Grounding allows you to be in charge as spirit.

THE SIXTH CHAKRA

The sixth chakra contains your information about clairvoyance. This chakra is located in the center of your head. Just as your physical eyes are located in your head, so your spiritual eye is also. The sixth chakra is shaped somewhat like a funnel, larger in front and quite small in back. It runs through your head parallel to the ground with the larger front at your forehead and the smaller back at the back of your head.

The sixth chakra is the appropriate place to be when you want to be neutral. It is the place to focus your attention when you want to see clearly or use your clairvoyance. The sixth chakra contains your clairvoyant information. The sixth chakra in the center of your head provides the most neutral perspective for you as spirit while in this physical world.

Since the sixth chakra contains our information about clairvoyance, it is the place to be, as spirit, if we wish to see clearly. The chakras below the sixth chakra are not appropriate levels to read from because they affect the view with inappropriate information. Lacking this awareness, you have most likely been focused in another chakra. It will take practice to learn to be in the sixth chakra.

Most people are taught by their families and society to focus in other chakras or outside of the body. Two common focuses are the fourth or heart chakra, which deals with affinity, and the second chakra, which deals with emotions. Either of these levels makes the individual vulnerable to being manipulated by others or his body, rather than allowing him to be neutral and in control of his information. By being in the sixth chakra, the individual can see what is happening and not be overwhelmed by the information in the other chakras, or by outside influences or his body.

When you focus your attention as spirit in the sixth chakra, you can use the information in this chakra and the information in all of the other chakras. Many of the chakras are overwhelming if you try to operate from within them. The other chakras color your view while the sixth is meant to be used to read from because it contains the information on clairvoyance or clear seeing. Clairvoyant information located in the sixth chakra allows you to lift the veil of the physical world and see spiritual reality. You can use your sixth chakra and clairvoyance to see auras, mental image pictures, symbols, formulas, beings without bodies and the other spiritual phenomena within and around you.

Often people will try to spiritually read from another chakra, such as the second chakra, which is located below the navel. The view from the second chakra does not provide a clear perspective since it contains information about our emotions and sexuality. Our clairsentience, or clear feeling, which is also located in the second chakra, can help us receive information about others, but it does not give us a neutral or clear perspective on the information it brings us.

If you or the person spiritually reading you state the information as "feeling" instead of "seeing," then the view is most likely from the second chakra. If the information is all of an emotional or sexual nature, the view is definitely from the second chakra. While some people believe this is all there is to life, it is only a very small part of life and needs to be kept in perspective. Moving out of the second chakra brings a broader view of reality.

By moving yourself and your attention up to the sixth chakra, in the center of your head, you change your view of life by activating your sixth chakra and seeing things from a spiritual perspective. You can still see the emotional, sexual aspects of your life, but they are in proportion. From the sixth chakra, you can see neutrally without being overwhelmed by your body or the messages from others' bodies.

You are a spiritual being abiding in a body. You are not bound by the limits of the body and can be anywhere in an instant. You can focus yourself into the center of your head and experience your clairvoyance. With this spiritual perspective, you can take charge of your life and see how to heal yourself, how you want to create and what you desire.

A friend spent several years discovering what he needed to do with his healing talents. He started by trying to use his healing abilities the way he believed others wanted him to, then he tried healing like someone he admired. Neither of these methods worked because he was not seeing himself clearly and being himself. It required the shock of losing his job for him to step back and use his clairvoyance to see himself and how he wanted to use his healing ability. He found a job focused exclusively on healing and has been happy being himself and healing ever since.

You can use your clairvoyance to know yourself, also. Your clairvoyance is a gift from God which needs to be treated with respect. When you ground and use the sixth chakra in a safe and healing manner, you allow respect for this gift. Let yourself get back in touch with this ability and the joy it can bring into your life, especially the joy of knowing yourself.

GROUND YOURSELF from your first chakra to the center of the Earth.

FOCUS YOURSELF as spirit into the center of your head. This is slightly above and behind your eyes. You will be wherever you put your attention, so simply put your attention behind your eyes.

YOU ARE a bright spark of light and can see yourself when you come into the center of your head.

USE YOUR INDEX FINGERS to help you locate the center of your head. Place one finger in the center of your forehead and one above and slightly in front of your ear. The center of your head is where imaginary lines from these fingers would intersect.

EXPERIENCE being in the center of your head and surrounded by your body. Notice your body's response to having you in the center of your head. Communicate to your body so it will feel safe having you, the energetic being, so focused in your head.

MOVE TO OTHER PLACES so you can get a clearer awareness of when you are in the center of your head and when you are somewhere else. Move to the top of your head. Move back to the center of your head.

SEE THE BRIGHT LIGHT that is you, the spirit, moving to these different places. Experience yourself, as spirit, separate from your body.

MOVE TO YOUR LEFT HAND and then back to the center of your head. Each time you leave the center of your head and return, notice how it feels to you and your body. Move to your right ear and then back to the center of your head.

MOVE TO THE AREA of your heart and experience being there. This may feel familiar. Be back in the center of your head.

USE YOUR GROUNDING to release any energy that was stimulated for you as you moved into different areas of your energy system.

The sixth chakra is located at the center of your head. Notice how your head feels when you focus your bright light there. Get acquainted with your sixth chakra. When you move into the center of your head, you awaken your sixth chakra.

By being in the center of your head, you stimulate the sixth chakra and your clairvoyance. An analogy can be made with the muscles in the body: if you use the muscles, they have greater strength. If you do not focus on them and use them, they become flaccid and out of shape. It is the same with your chakras: if you focus on them and use them, you stimulate growth and strength.

Whenever you focus on and use any aspect of your energy system, you strengthen it. Since the sixth chakra contains your information about clairvoyance, you strengthen your ability to see clearly when you focus in the center of your head and awaken your sixth chakra.

The gland associated with the sixth chakra is the pineal gland. It is located at the top of the spinal column near the center of your head. The pineal gland is a reflector of light and can be used to reflect your bright light as spirit.

It is helpful to be at your pineal gland when you meditate since this stimulates your clairvoyance and reflects your light. When you focus in the sixth chakra and on the pineal gland, you stimulate this ability to reflect light and see clearly. You need to be in your sixth chakra for daily living, but do not need to focus as much on your pineal gland unless you are meditating. Focusing in your sixth chakra can be an adventure and a joy.

CREATE YOUR GROUNDING CORD from your first chakra to the center of the Earth, and focus in the center of your head. As you focus your energy here, get the concept that you are activating your sixth chakra.

INCREASE YOUR GROUNDING. Put your attention on your pineal gland. Get the concept of putting the bright light that is you on the pineal and gently stimulating the pineal gland. Release any excess energy down your grounding cord.

NOTICE how this affects you and your body. Listen to your body's response to you focusing your attention so strongly.

ALLOW ANY UNWANTED ENERGY to flow down your grounding cord. Release any unpleasant emotions down your grounding cord. Enhance your grounding to help you to feel safe while you activate your sixth chakra.

The sixth chakra, which runs through the center of your head, contains your information on clairvoyance and is the place you can most easily experience neutrality. When you are neutral, you do not judge yourself or others. Using clairvoyance allows you to see clearly and from neutral, which allows you not to judge.

EXPERIENCE your neutrality now. Sit straight in your chair, so your energy runs smoothly. Separate your hands and have your feet on the floor. Focus your attention into the center of your head. Create the connection between your first chakra, near the base of your spine, and the center of the Earth.

TAKE A DEEP BREATH, and relax your body. You need to communicate with your body to create harmony with it. Be in the neutral place in the sixth chakra, in the center of your head, and remember an issue in your life you wish to change. Notice how you are viewing this experience. Are you seeing only the physical aspect?

TAKE ANOTHER DEEP BREATH, and allow yourself to see the issue from this neutral place and gain a spiritual perspective. Ask yourself what you, as spirit, are trying to learn from this experience. Allow yourself to see how you can best learn the lesson for which you created this situation. You may be surprised at the answer. Often we believe that the way we are viewing a situation is the only possible way, when, in fact, it is not. You may realize that all you need to do is something as simple as changing your view of the scene.

LET INTERFERENCE TO SEEING your lesson go down your grounding cord. Release any interference to learning your lesson down your grounding cord.

LOOK AT THE ISSUE from neutral, and notice any change in your perspective.

For example, you may be judging someone and wanting to let go of the judgement. Look at your judgement of this person from neutral, and get a new perspective. You may see a past life where the other person failed to help you and you judged him as unfaithful. You may be together again to complete this cycle, and you may be continuing to judge the other person for not living up to your expectations. When you get in neutral, you can forgive him for being human and having human faults. You may realize that you would behave similarly if you were in the same situation. With neutrality, you can see the other person's better qualities and that you and your friend have a lot in common.

Often your need to judge is a need to make yourself a good person and someone else a bad one. This need to be right or good is a trait you may not like but need to recognize so you can free yourself from this pattern. When you look at life from neutral, you can allow yourself and others to be human instead of expecting everyone to be perfect.

BE GROUNDED, and focus in the sixth chakra. Look at one of your creations which you do not like. Look at your judgement of this creation. Clear the judgement by letting it go down your grounding cord.

ALLOW YOUR SPIRITUAL PERSPECTIVE by being aware that you are not your creation. Allow yourself to be separate from your creation. From the center of your head, see what you need to do to relate to this creation from neutral. Release energy down your grounding cord that stops the healing. By grounding and being in the sixth chakra, you do not identify yourself with your creation and can be neutral about it, which gives you control and the power to change it.

ALLOW THE EMOTIONAL ENERGY about the creation to go down your grounding cord. Let yourself see the situation from neutral. Allow time to release the emotions of your body.

When you allow yourself to practice this simple technique of looking at problems as lessons, your perspective moves to the spiritual realm and your neutrality increases. You can then make more mature decisions while lifted above the emotional turmoil which you have created. Each time you have a decision you are having difficulty with, sit quietly, ground and focus into the center of your head. Then see spiritually what you have created and how you can best learn from the experience. This simple practice will change your outlook on life. You can be in conscious control as spirit, instead of allowing your body or others to be in charge of you.

It is beneficial to open and use the sixth chakra before you open the other chakras. You see what you are doing when you open the other centers if you have developed your sixth chakra. All spiritual work is enhanced by your clairvoyance.

The joy you can get from seeing your spiritual creativity makes the process of opening your sixth chakra well worth the time and energy spent. The spiritual information located in the sixth chakra can be of great benefit to you and to everyone with whom you come in contact.

Figure 1: Sixth Chakra

VISUALIZATION

You are a unique spiritual being creating your personal experience. You create your life from your desires and your beliefs. Your ability to visualize what you want assists you to make your beliefs and desires manifest in the physical realm. Visualization is a technique which uses your clairvoyance to create your life.

You may use your clairvoyance to see what is, what will be or what has been. Visualization is seeing what you want to create. When you visualize something, you see your creation made manifest. Visualization is a creative aspect of your clairvoyance.

You, as spirit, can create anything you desire and believe you can create. Visualizing what you want helps you create it in the physical world. It is similar to painting a picture or creating graphics on your computer. You, as spirit, consciously create what you desire on an energy level and then allow it time to manifest physically.

I was happy to see a student I had not seen for a year. In my greeting, I asked her where she had been, and she told me she took a break from the training because the power of her creativity frightened her. She visualized what she wanted, and it happened. She visualized the car she wanted, a vacation to Hawaii, her ideal job and all of these things manifested in her life. She then visualized her ideal mate, and he materialized in a few months. She is still adjusting to all that she consciously created using visualization.

You can use visualization to gain conscious control of your creativity. Instead of being unaware of what you are doing, you can visualize what you desire and use the techniques to help you create it. You can visualize both spiritual and physical creations.

The symbol of a rose is a neutral symbol often used in the visualization process. Because a rose is neutral, it is easy to use in all of our creative visualization. The rose is neither positive nor negative and seldom causes strong emotional reactions. It is a symbol of purity and neutrality that has been used through the ages to represent and assist with spiritual opening and development. Like the lotus in Eastern religions, the rose represents the opening of the soul to God.

CREATE YOUR GROUNDING cord from your first chakra to the center of the Earth. Focus, as spirit, into the center of your head. Allow your body to adjust to your grounding and to you in the center of your head.

FROM THE CENTER OF YOUR HEAD, visualize a rose approximately six inches in front of your forehead. Take a moment and admire your creation. You have created the mental image picture of a rose.

FROM THE CENTER of your head, let the rose in front of you disappear. You can let it melt away or you can explode it like a firecracker. By letting the rose go, you create room to create another rose. Create another rose and admire this one. Explode the rose and admire your ability to change.

By releasing the rose, you free the energy you used to create it to create another rose. Energy is never destroyed. It is transformed. When you use your clairvoyance to see what you are creating and destroying in your life, you take charge of the creation of your life. When you work in the dark without your clairvoyant skills, you make unnecessary mistakes and create unneeded misery for yourself and others.

Your clairvoyance opens your awareness to what you are creating and allows you to be consciously aware of your choices. Without your spiritual sight, you can easily be confused and manipulated. Your ability to visualize allows you to take charge of your creativity and direct your energy. You can create an image, see it and allow it to manifest; or you can let it go. You can use your clairvoyance to visualize a rose and use the rose to help you change and create your life.

BE GROUNDED and in the center of your head. Visualize a rose six inches in front of your forehead and then let go of the rose. Notice how your body feels when you do this.

PRACTICE CREATING and letting go of roses for a few moments to experience the power of this spiritual technique. Use your grounding to help your body feel safe, and release energy as you use this spiritual power in your body.

Using this technique of creating and exploding roses, while being grounded and in the center of your head, helps you take conscious control of your life. It stimulates your sixth chakra and the other apparatus connected with your clairvoyant abilities. It also cleanses your spiritual system and enhances your grounding.

You can use the visualization of the rose as a way to help you see yourself and others more clearly. You can have the rose represent you or someone else and see the spiritual nature of either. For example, you can visualize a rose to represent your present state of being and interpret the rose to help you see yourself as spirit. You may see a bright green rose representing you and interpret it as a symbol of the major growth process you are in. It can also be used as a healing tool in connection with your clairvoyance. You can use the rose to see your state of being and to release energy you do not wish to keep to change your experience. You can do this by simply creating and letting go of the rose to release the unwanted energy and create the desired change.

GROUND, CENTER and create and destroy roses. Be aware of how your forehead feels, how your head feels. Notice if you physically feel anything in your head. By being aware as you create and explode roses, you validate your experience. Create a rose, let any unwanted energy in your head flow out into the rose, and explode the rose and the energy. Notice how your head feels now.

INCREASE YOUR GROUNDING, and be in the center of your head. Create a rose in front of you. Be aware of one issue in your life about which you do not feel in control. Let this issue go out into your rose. Explode the issue in the rose, and create another rose and explode it. Continue to visualize creating and exploding the issue in the rose several times. The more emotional you are about the issue, the more time it will require to clear energy around this issue.

ALLOW ENERGY to be released down your grounding cord. Release any sense of a lack of control about the issue as you create and explode roses.

BE CENTERED and grounded. Explode a final rose. Take a deep breath, and visualize how you can take control of this experience.

By using your clairvoyance and your ability to visualize, you clear the issue. This technique requires faith. All spiritual work requires faith. It is necessary for you to let go of your intellectual limits and use your spiritual abilities for results to occur.

BE GROUNDED and in the center of your head. Be aware of a relationship you wish to heal, such as one between you and a friend.

CREATE A ROSE in front of you, and let the energy disturbing your relationship go into the rose. Explode the rose. Create and destroy the rose with the disturbance in it until you see that the disturbance is gone.

If you do not see clairvoyantly yet, allow yourself to know when you are finished with the healing.

VISUALIZE a rose for a healed relationship and release it, so it can be physically manifested. Allow yourself to spiritually create what you want.

Clairvoyance brings light and perspective to every area of life. By using it to visualize what you want and to cleanse what you do not want, it helps you heal yourself and your creations.

By using visualization, we take conscious control of our creativity. We can visualize the desired result and then visualize removing all barriers to this end. We can visualize the healing desired and use the techniques to bring about what we want. The ability to visualize is a way of creating spiritually in the physical world.

When we use our visualization, our ability to see spiritually, and our neutrality, we are practicing our clairvoyance. We can learn to see what is and what we want and be neutral about both in order to bring about the change we wish. This brings clarity, healing, power and the joy of being in charge of our own creative process.

"Your clairvoyance
opens your awareness
to what you are creating
and allows you to be
consciously aware of
your choices... Your
ability to visualize
allows you to take
charge of your creativity
and direct your energy."

Truth/Lie Rose

Your clairvoyance allows you to tell a truth from a lie. This ability is valuable in every aspect of your life. It can help you with both your spiritual and physical creativity. However, you may find that some people do not want you to use this skill because they want you to believe their lies in order to control you. It is fascinating and often disturbing to discover how many people in your life lie to you. It can also be fun to watch as people realize that you know they are lying. You need to add yourself into your new observations to see how often you lie to yourself and others. When you see how much you lie, you may find that a truth is more effective in creating what you want.

Everyone lies about something. Our facades are lies. We lie to protect our ego. Our desire for perfection is a lie because perfection is not part of our experience as human beings. We lie to feel we have an advantage. We lie to cover mistakes. We lie about so many things that most people have lost track of the fact that they are lying. The ability to tell a truth from a lie is most helpful in getting back on track in this world. We have darkened our world with so many lies that we need to begin to see the lies in order to heal.

The ability to see a lie and see a truth is an obvious asset in anyone's life. It can be helpful in any circumstance, from buying a used car to choosing a life partner. This aspect of clairvoyance can be used in healing, business, relationships and all parts of one's life. The question is why more people do not want to know the truth.

It appears that many people prefer to stay in the dark about things and fool themselves that things are the way they wish them to be, instead of the way they are. If you see that shiny, new-looking used car and it is just as you pictured it, you may not want to see that the engine is not good. If you see the truth, then you would be foolish to buy the car. By allowing yourself to see that the salesperson is lying to you about the quality of the vehicle, you can save yourself a good deal of grief that would come from trying to make the car into what you believed it was. By not purchasing the car, you do have to keep looking, but you save yourself money, time and energy that would have been spent in trying to improve the faulty car.

This analogy could be related to choosing a mate. If we see the other person as he or she is, we know what we are getting. When we buy his or her facades and lies, we are disappointed when he or she does not live up to those images or our expectations. Seeing the truth and the lie allows us to navigate safely through life because we are not constantly falling over surprises that come from accepting a lie.

A friend of mine has a chronic problem of not only accepting lies about women, but also of creating lies about them himself. He is attracted to the brightest and most beautiful women who are swept off of their feet by his masculine power. He believes their lies that they will be subservient to him, and he also believes his lies that they are perfect. Time always brings these lies to the light of truth, and he is once again alone and searching for his image of a perfect woman, which is a lie.

The technique of telling a truth from a lie can be helpful in creating a happy life because it helps you avoid some wrong choices. My friend refuses to see himself and his own lies which makes it difficult for him to see other people's lies. It is an asset to turn within and know yourself when learning what is a truth and what is a lie so you can operate from your information and not someone else's.

Practice your ability to tell a truth from a lie. If you practice in simple situations, you will build your confidence. You may want to practice on information you already know. If you are extremely emotional about an issue, it will be more difficult for you to see clearly, so choose easy issues to begin. You will eventually become proficient and can use this technique in any circumstance.

SIT IN A STRAIGHT-BACKED CHAIR with your feet on the floor and your hands separated in your lap. Close your eyes and turn your attention within to the center of your head. Take a few deep breaths to relax your body.

GROUND YOURSELF from your first chakra to the center of the Earth, and allow the energy flowing down your grounding cord to carry away any unwanted energy. Let your grounding clear away any foreign energy.

FROM YOUR SIXTH CHAKRA, in the center of your head, visualize the image of a rose six inches in front of your forehead. Explode the rose. Create another rose and explode it. Repeat creating and exploding roses to clear your sixth chakra.

BE GROUNDED and in the center of your head. Create a rose in front of you. Think of something you know to be true, and watch the rose. Think of something you know to be a lie, and watch the rose.

The rose will remain unchanged if the statement is true. The rose will change in some way if it is a lie. The rose may shake, turn dark, fall over, or disappear, but it will change in some way. You can practice this technique with several truths and lies to increase your confidence and proficiency. Keep the exercise fun and light to begin with and you will develop this skill easily.

GROUND, and be in the center of your head. Create and explode roses again to clear your sixth chakra. Use your grounding to release any unwanted energy from your body and energy system.

FROM THIS NEUTRAL SPACE, see a lie you have been telling yourself. Put the lie in a rose, and explode the rose until the lie is gone. Allow yourself to see what is true for you, and create and explode roses to clear any barrier to having this truth.

BE GROUNDED and in the center of your head. Create a rose about six inches in front of your forehead. Think of something you are being told by someone else. If the rose changes, it is a lie. Explode the rose.

CREATE AND EXPLODE ROSES, and use your grounding cord to release the emotions and other energies that emerge as you begin to see the truth from the lie.

You can use this technique to see lies that you tell yourself and lies that others tell you. Be aware of being in neutral, so you do not get caught in judging yourself or the other people. Seeing the truth for yourself helps you create your clear personal path.

We all tell lies because we have come to believe some of them are truth. This simple technique can help us tell a truth from a lie. Then it is up to us to be neutral about what we see. With this new awareness, we regain our power and have a clearer view of how to create in this world.

When you begin to see the truth and the lie, it can create a growth experience for you and your body. It is helpful to use the techniques to cleanse whatever this exercise stimulates in your system. Grounding and being in the center of your head help you be safe and neutral. The next technique of running energies helps you cleanse unwanted energy, keep the system clear of lies and balance spirit and body.

When you use this technique to see the truth with neutrality and a spiritual perspective, it can bring you joy and freedom. Like all things, if you use it with judgement, fear and anger, it will bring you pain and unhappiness. Everyone has her own truth. When you allow your truth, you give others permission to do the same. Everything in your life is up to you. You can create with joy and healing or with whatever you choose.

As spirit, we love truth. Bodies often become dependent on lies, believing they need the lie to survive. By using the spiritual techniques and increasing our awareness, we enhance our spiritual creativity, communication and power. We take seniority over the body and the physical world.

Allow yourself the spiritual perspective of truth. See the truth and "the truth will set you free."

Cosmic
Energy

Earth
Energy

Grounding Cord

Figure 2: Running Energy

RUNNING ENERGY

All things are composed of energy in motion. Our energies are already moving through us. By consciously manipulating our energies, we gain control of the flow of vibrations and create greater awareness of our system and creativity.

There are many energies available for us to use. The ones we will work with are earth and cosmic energies. These represent our spiritual and physical natures and help us to be in touch with both the spiritual and physical aspects of our creativity.

The earth energy is the vibration of the planet Earth. We can draw upon this energy to be in touch with the physical world. Earth energy helps us to relate to and create through our physical world. Our bodies are part of the Earth's energies.

Cosmic energy is the infinite energy of the Cosmos. It is available for us to use to create as spirit. We can use it to enhance our clairvoyance, healing and other spiritual abilities. We can use different vibrations of cosmic energy to heal ourselves, to see more clearly and to create a spiritually focused life.

Consciously running energy helps develop clairvoyance because it is a way of cleansing the energy system. The clearer we make our system, the more clearly we experience our abilities, including clairvoyance. When you run your energy, you cleanse and activate all of the chakras. This cleansing and stimulation of the sixth chakra increases your clairvoyance.

Your clairvoyance is an asset as you run your energy because it helps you see where you need to focus your attention. When you focus your attention on something, you can use the earth and cosmic energy to melt unwanted energy away to cleanse your system in order to enhance a strength. You can also begin to see foreign energy in your system and can remove it to help your energy flow more freely. Running your energy helps you balance spirit and body, so you can harmonize as you create.

Experience running your energy now as you practice your other techniques. Practice helps you to be proficient with the techniques. The more you use the techniques, the greater your focus on your spiritual perspective.

GROUND and be in the center of your head. Take a few deep breaths to relax your body. Settle your body in a comfortable position with your spine as straight as possible, your feet on the floor and your hands separated in your lap. Your energy runs more smoothly when your spine is straight.

FROM THIS GROUNDED, CENTERED POSITION, be aware of your feet on the floor. There are chakras in the arches of your feet. Open these chakras, and allow the earth energy to flow up through the foot chakras, into the channels in the legs and through the leg channels to the first chakra, near the base of the spine.

ALLOW THE EARTH ENERGY to flow down your grounding cord. This flow of earth energy, up through the foot chakras and leg channels, to the first chakra and down the grounding cord, enhances your grounding and puts you in touch with the Earth.

BE GROUNDED and in the center of your head, and let the earth energy flow. Create and explode roses to clear any interference to this flow of earth energy.

FROM THE CENTER of your head, activate your sixth chakra, and look at the flow of your earth energy. If there is a block to this flow of energy, focus the earth energy there, and let it melt away the unwanted energy. You can also create and explode roses to release the energy stopping the flow.

EXPERIENCE the smooth flow of earth energy. Be still in the center of your head, and be aware of the impact of this energy on you and your body. Enjoy its healing effect.

Earth energy is a powerful force, as exemplified in volcanos, floods, hurricanes and other powerful Earth changes. It needs to be used gently to allow for the desired clearing and healing. When used consistently and gently, it has the power of water on rock which smooths and polishes. The Grand Canyon is a wonderful example of the power of a flow of energy in the form of water. Earth energy is a great power available to us for our creative and healing process. Just as plants use the Earth to grow, we can use the energy of the Earth to grow and heal. Our clairvoyance can help us see how to use it.

Cosmic energy is the spiritual balance for earth energy. Cosmic energy is made up of all vibrations. It is all light. We can use any of the cosmic vibrations for our work here on Earth. In this exercise, we use gold energy as it is a neutral, healing energy.

GROUND, be in the center of your head, and run your earth energy up through the foot chakras and the leg channels, to your first chakra and down the grounding cord.

CREATE A BALL OF BRIGHT GOLD energy above your head. Let the energy flow down to the top of your head and down channels along each side of your spine. Allow the energy to come to your first chakra and mix with the earth energy. Bring the mixture of mostly cosmic energy and some earth energy up through channels in your body. Allow the energy to flow gently up through the channels running through the entire body. Let the energy fountain out the top of your head and flow all around you. Allow some of the energy to flow from the cleft of your throat down your arms and out your hands.

BE GROUNDED and centered, and enjoy the flow of earth and cosmic energies through your system. Take time to experience these energies running through your channels.

FROM YOUR SIXTH CHAKRA, see if there is any interference to the flow of your cosmic energy. If you see interference, use the cosmic energy to melt the obstruction away. Use your grounding to release the energy from your system.

BE IN YOUR SIXTH CHAKRA, and look for any foreign energy in your cosmic energy channels: back, front or arm channels. If you see any foreign energy, create and explode roses to release the energy from your system. You can also use your grounding cord to release the energy, or let the flow of cosmic energy melt the foreign energy away.

SIT QUIETLY in the center of your head, and be grounded while you run your cosmic and earth energies. Allow a time of peace and quiet, and enjoy the healing flow.

The more you run your energies, the greater control you will have of your creativity on this Earth. Your use of the cosmic and earth energies to cleanse yourself increases your clarity and your ability to see. Running your energies for thirty minutes a day can bring you clarity. You will find the time spent in meditation well worth it.

Using your clairvoyance, together with grounding and running energies, creates a powerful healing process. It can put you in charge of your life. By using your spiritual skills, you operate as spirit and experience the power and joy of creating and communicating as spirit.

THE AURA

All things have an aura. The aura is an energy field which indicates one's present state of being, such as health or illness, anger or joy, oneness or separation and so forth. If the aura is bright and clear, there is spiritual and physical health. If the aura is dark and cloudy, there is disturbance. Being aware of the aura is a great benefit in healing as well as in communicating and creating our reality.

The aura can be seen clairvoyantly as colors which represent vibrations. The color itself is not as significant as the state of the vibration. Clarity or murkiness is more significant than the color. For example, red can be translated into many meanings depending on its lightness or darkness. A light, bright red could indicate life force energy. Dark, cloudy red could indicate stuck anger. Being aware of the state of the vibration, rather than intellectualizing the color, brings more information about the aura.

By looking clairvoyantly at your aura, you can read your state of being. You then have the information needed to change anything you need to heal. Your view from the sixth chakra not only helps you to see the aura, but also helps you to avoid judgement about what you see. If you see what is and then respond to the situation from neutral, you have power over your creativity.

The aura ideally comes all around your body. It comes under your feet, above your head and equidistant all around your body. If the aura is not all the way under your feet, it indicates that you are not manifesting your spiritual energy all the way into your body. If it is too close to your back, it indicates you do not own your back. People who do not have their aura around their back feel a need to protect their back, thus the old saying of keeping your back to the wall. The body feels safer when you have your aura all the way around it.

Seeing your aura provides you with a wealth of information to help you heal yourself. If you see that it is not all around you, you can use the techniques to adjust your aura so it goes all around your body. This spiritual ownership of your body and energy system helps you more fully and consciously create in both the physical and spiritual realms.

Your aura shows you and others the perimeter of your spiritual space. It is your God-given space in which you are meant to create. To maintain control of your aura, or space, keep your aura six to twelve inches around your body. This allows you to be the only one within your space and makes it easy for you to control. If you expand your aura to include others, you experience their creativity also. This includes their emotions, ethics, beliefs and so forth.

We all expand our aura in certain circumstances, so we have to learn to bring our aura back to ourselves. This learning process helps us to regain control of our aura and our space as we consciously manipulate our energy. The aura can be expanded and contracted without any limit. We can contract it to the size of the body, or much less, and expand it to the size of the universe. The goal is to learn to be in control of it, and this is best experienced when it is close to the body.

Playing with your aura during your meditations can be fun. It helps you learn how you feel with it expanded or contracted, so you know what you are doing. Looking at your aura can help you understand yourself in a new way and explain many things you previously found mysterious.

GROUND from your first chakra to the center of the Earth. Focus yourself into the center of your head. Be aware of your aura.

SEE IF YOUR AURA is all around your body. If it is not, bring it under your feet, above your head and equally around the front and back of your body. Be in the center of your head and grounded, and experience your aura all the way around you. Breathe deeply to help your energy flow.

FROM THIS GROUNDED, NEUTRAL space, create and explode roses and watch your aura. By creating and exploding roses, you relax and cleanse your aura. Take a few minutes to do this and see the results. It is possible to change the vibration from dense to clear by grounding and creating and releasing roses.

EXPERIENCE manipulating your aura. Ground, be in your sixth chakra and be aware of your aura around you. Expand your aura to fill the room. Notice how this feels. Contract your aura to six inches around your body and notice how this feels.

You have greater control when you have your aura within six to twelve inches around you. If you expand your aura and someone else is in the room with you, you will experience his reality as well as yours. This can be confusing and will disrupt your personal system.

FROM THE CENTER of your head, ground, and be aware of your aura within six to twelve inches all around your body. Look at your aura from the sixth chakra. See the state of your aura. Is it clear?

ALLOW any cloudy or dark energy to flow from your aura down your grounding cord. Continue to release the energy until your aura becomes clear and bright.

CREATE and explode roses to expedite this cleansing of your aura.

BE AWARE of how your body feels when you cleanse your aura. Notice how cleansing affects your grounding and your ability to focus in the center of your head.

The aura has many different vibrations in it. We need to focus on the main ones in order to heal ourselves. There are usually seven main vibrations which relate to the seven main chakras. There is no correct set of vibrations to maintain in your aura. Each soul is unique and has unique lessons, so each aura is unique. The aura changes according to the state of the being and the experience of the present moment.

It is helpful to read your aura to see what you are creating and if you need to make any adjustments to your system. You can do this focused in your sixth chakra where you are neutral about yourself and your creations.

CREATE YOUR GROUNDING cord from your first chakra to the center of the Earth. Focus in your sixth chakra. Be aware of your aura all around your body.

LOOK AT YOUR AURA. See the vibration that is closest to your body. Translate the vibration to a color. Translate the color to a few words. You are translating spiritual information to physical understanding.

USE YOUR GROUNDING CORD to release any unwanted energy. Create and explode roses to cleanse that layer of your aura.

By reading yourself, you get to know you as spirit. Reading yourself could go somewhat as follows: if you saw a vibration and translated it to blue and translated that to healing your relationship with your body, you could get some validation about the attention you are putting on your physical health. Or, if you saw dark red and translated that into anger, it could let you know that your body is angry with you about the way you are relating to it.

Another example would be if you see a dark yellow and interpret this as how you relate to the Earth through your intellectual limits and programming. By releasing the darkness in the vibration, you can bring it to a bright, light yellow and relate to the Earth through joy. The best way to learn to read yourself is to do it. If you practice, you will eventually learn your way of reading yourself. The secret is to practice.

GROUND, CENTER and look at the next vibration out from your body. Translate this into a color and into a few words. Use your grounding to release energy. Create and explode roses to cleanse your aura.

CONTINUE LOOKING at each layer of your aura up to seven and translating the vibration to color and the color into words.

GROUND AWAY the unwanted energy from each layer and create and explode roses to assist the cleansing process.

Record the information in a journal to help you validate all you see. You may find it helpful to take notes so you can remember what you have seen. If you keep this information, you will see patterns that will help you know yourself. The more you know, see and understand yourself, the greater control you have over your creativity. See yourself, and you free yourself from manipulation by others, by your body's desires and by the lies you have accepted and created in this world.

Reading your aura can be a regular part of your meditations and self healing sessions. You may also find it helpful to have another reader give you information because another person can often see things you cannot see about yourself. If you are too emotional about issues, you will not see them clearly.

By seeing your state of being, you can know yourself and heal yourself. By using your clairvoyance, you can have greater control of your life and a lot more fun because you see what you are doing.

First Chakra

Grounding Cord

Figure 3: The Aura

Clairvoyance and Healing

Clairvoyance is an important ingredient in healing. Since healing requires change, you need to see what is occurring before you decide what to change. When you use your clairvoyance, you can see clearly what you need to do. If you do not use this ability, you are working in the dark. It is like driving your car with a blindfold on or performing an operation in the dark.

Healing is change, so you need to see what needs changing before you begin healing. If you are dealing with healing a relationship, you need to see what to change within yourself, since you cannot change anything in another person. To determine what you want to change, you need to see yourself from neutral so that you do not let judgement stop your healing process. By using your clairvoyance, you see yourself clearly, from neutral, and can decide what you want to do. When you operate from a spiritual perspective, your decisions are made from a position of neutral power, instead of from an emotional state. You can use your clairvoyant ability to see what you need to change and how to best create the healing.

An important aspect of neutrality is validating yourself. You can heal easily when you accept yourself as you are. Your clairvoyance helps you see yourself so you can validate what is. I have a friend who is extremely talented, but he does not validate his talents. He is engulfed in other people's criticism of him and his own loneliness because he believes he is not as good as others. He is actually more capable than most of the people around him who invalidate him to manipulate him into giving to them.

Recently, my friend started an intense healing process using these techniques and his clairvoyance. He changed his life drastically in ten months. The main change came from his validation of himself. He began to see himself as a bright, powerful soul with the ability to create whatever he wanted. He left his old friends and developed new friendships. He improved his business. He experienced liking himself and being happy. A major lesson for this man was validating himself as spirit and how capable he was. It is an important step for all of us to see and love our bright, powerful selves.

Your life lessons are part of your spiritual healing process. Clairvoyance can help you learn your lessons in a healing manner and to learn to validate yourself as you are. When you can see clearly, healing is easier and more fun.

GROUND from your first chakra to the center of the Earth. Use your grounding to establish a safe space for your work.

BE IN THE CENTER of your head and use your clairvoyance. Visualize a rose and explode the rose. Create another rose, and allow yourself to see a lesson you are learning in this life.

ALLOW YOUR NEUTRALITY to help you see what you are trying to learn. It may be something you do not like. Nevertheless, it is your lesson, and it is necessary for you to see it to learn it most effectively. Allow any judgement to go down your grounding cord, and let yourself see the lesson from neutral.

CREATE A ROSE and move the lesson into the rose. Create and explode the rose with the lesson in it several times to clear any foreign energy from it. Explode the rose a final time.

BE IN THE CENTER of your head and be grounded. Visualize a rose in front of you and let it go. Create another rose, and allow any energy stopping you from learning your lesson to go into the rose. Explode the rose and the interference. Create and explode several roses for this one interference to your healing.

CONTINUE TO GROUND, be in the center of your head and run your earth and cosmic energies. Allow the flow of energy to wash away any interference to you learning this lesson. Let the unwanted energy go down your grounding cord.

BE GROUNDED AND CENTERED, and give yourself permission to learn your lesson. Be aware that this will create a growth experience for you and that your life will change.

When you use your clairvoyance to see yourself and what you are learning as spirit, you are better able to control your life. If you are learning humility this lifetime, it would explain why you constantly create humiliating circumstances to help you learn the lesson. If you see that you need to learn this quality, you can consciously develop it and no longer need to create difficulties through which to learn. Once you learn that lesson, you can move on to other lessons.

By using your clairvoyance, you can see the lesson instead of fighting it. Clarity helps you to see things as they are and to control the body's desire to fight or flee the creation. If something frightens the body, it believes it must run or fight to be safe. This fight or flight instinct is one you can learn to control when you use your clairvoyance because you can see what is and deal with it in a neutral, spiritual manner.

We store our memories in the form of mental image pictures which we can see with our clairvoyance.

Experiences in the present can stimulate these memories so they surface from the subsconscious and affect our present behavior. These memories can create irrational behavior in the present because we operate on the information from the memory pictures instead of from the present circumstances. We can use our clairvoyance to see the pictures and our spiritual techniques to clear emotion from them so we can be in control of our present circumstances.

Non-resistance is another spiritual skill that is helpful in healing. It is the ability to let energy pass through or by you without affecting you. This skill of non-resistance is enhanced by your clairvoyance. When you can see what is, you do not feel you need to fight or flee. When you do not resist, you can take charge and change the situation. You can learn to be non-resistant to energy from others and to your energy from the past or energy based on lies.

A friend of mine is a great fighter and has used resistance to create his life. He changed this pattern over time by using the techniques and his clairvoyance to heal himself. His childhood was a violent experience, so his healing process involved violence until he learned he could use non-resistance instead of struggling. He was so programmed to grow through pain that he continued that pattern in healing for quite awhile. Fortunately, the aspect of violence diminished rapidly until he ceased to create violent conflict situations. He is now able to laugh at himself about how well he can resist. His amusement helps him let go of his past patterns and use his new spiritual techniques.

He is a good example of how much we can get caught in the body's survival instincts of fight or flight and how this causes us to resist. You can use your clairvoyance to see your patterns of resistance, and you can change them and be able to simply be, as spirit. My friend enjoys life a great deal more now that he is able to let things go instead of resisting so much. He is much more in charge of his creativity.

Your clairvoyance is a great asset in developing your non-resistance because it lets you see what is. With clear sight, you can navigate smoothly through life without having to fight and struggle. Non-resistance can help you let go of unwanted energies and alter circumstances. When you resist something, it sticks to you. If you do not resist, it passes through you and does not affect you. Since the instinct of the body to fight for its survival is so strong, this is a technique that takes time to develop. You can develop it by using your techniques of grounding, being in the center of your head, and running your energy. Creating and letting go of roses also helps you let go.

GROUND and be in the center of your head. Be aware of something in your life that you are resisting. You may be resisting a person, emotion or situation.

FROM THE CENTER OF YOUR HEAD, see what is causing you to resist. It could be fear, a past experience or anything. Create a rose in front of you and release whatever is causing you to resist into the rose and explode the rose.

REPEAT CREATING AND LETTING GO of the rose several times to release the energy. Use your grounding cord to release the resistance from your body.

NOTICE how your body feels after you release the resistance. Be grounded and centered, create and explode roses and readjust your energy system.

By running your energy and using the other techniques, you develop your non-resistance. You cleanse the things that cause you to resist, such as pain, fear, doubt, hate or whatever you have created in your life that triggers your resistance. Using your clairvoyance to see the issues from a spiritual perspective helps you rise above the emotions that cause you to resist.

Often we need to deal with something which occurred in our past in order to heal in the present. When we see clairvoyantly, we can see the issue and use our spiritual techniques to clear the emotions and energy of the past experience. Our clairvoyance helps us refrain from fighting or running and assists us to be still and respond as spirit to the situation.

There are many times when people find themselves running away, or wanting to run away, from something and they do not know the cause of their behavior. The reason for this desire to flee can be from a memory of an experience from the past. By using clairvoyance, one can see the disturbance and then use the techniques of grounding, exploding roses and running energy to clear it instead of reacting with inappropriate behavior.

An example of this phenomenon is a woman who keeps running from one relationship to another because she is afraid of men. By turning within and using her clairvoyance, she could see what is really causing her body to be afraid. It could be a childhood experience that gave her reason to be afraid of men. By seeing the experience and then clearing it, she frees herself to create her adult life as she wishes instead of attempting to run from something that is not in the present, but in her past.

We often recreate circumstances until we learn a lesson. The woman may have created relationships with men in her adult life similar to what she had experienced as a child and thereby perpetuated her fear. It also could be that the physical characteristics of a man reminded her of the past experience, though his nature is different. A partner may be loving and kind and still stimulate a past experience because he smokes a pipe or has a beard or shares some other seemingly meaningless thing with the person who frightened her in the past.

The healing occurs when the woman looks clearly at herself and realizes that she is running away from something in herself. When she stops and faces her own creations, she can make clear decisions about her present circumstances and cease to make the same mistakes. By using her clairvoyance, she sees her patterns and can heal herself. She can let go of the past and create in the present.

A friend of mine was sexually abused as a child. She recreated this abuse throughout her youth and young adulthood because her image of herself, her beliefs and her habits kept her involved with abusive men. She discovered these meditation techniques and used her clairvoyance to heal herself. She clearly saw the abusive experiences in her past as she consciously brought them to the surface. She even ran away from her healing one time, but returned to her task and continued to heal her past.

After several years of spiritual work, she was able to create a loving marriage and a family. As she continued her spiritual healing work, her past pain continued to surface for her to clear from her system. Her clairvoyance allowed her to see and let go of the intense fear and hate that accompanied the painful creations. Her spiritual work has made it possible for her to be a loving wife and mother and to regain control over her creations.

In most of our healing processes and lessons, we involve other souls. We have agreements with other souls that vary from helping each other for a few moments to being together for many lifetimes. Everyone we associate with stimulates our growth and reflects our characteristics. Our clairvoyance helps us see how others affect us, how we affect others and how we can best use the interaction to heal ourselves and others.

Our spiritual agreements are an important part of our creativity and our learning process. Whom we choose to be with has a major influence on our lives. If we choose loving people, it can enhance this quality in us. The other souls we agree to work with in a lifetime are like mirrors for us to use to read ourselves. Clairvoyance can help us look within to create change, rather than trying to change those around us. We cannot change others. We can change ourselves.

Agreements can be changed. You may sign papers to buy a house and years later sell the house; you get married and divorced; you make agreements and change them. For example, we may choose a group of physically focused souls to begin life with in order to learn about this world. We may then develop our spiritual awareness and move on to a group which is spiritually focused, leaving the original group. Each group is part of the learning, healing process of the individual. The soul makes agreements with each group and ends or changes the agreements as it matures.

A soul may need to learn a lesson about something horrible. The soul can heal through the lesson in this life or a future life. In his youth, the man who wrote the hymn "Amazing Grace" was involved in the slave trade. Later in his life, he became a minister and was a major influence in abolishing slavery in England. We all have some lessons to move through, even if they are not this extreme. The people we agree to work with are a reflection of where we are and what we need to learn to progress and grow. We may play many parts in a play before we learn the lesson provided by the play. We make agreements to interact with others to help us learn.

If you do not like someone in your life, you can use your clairvoyance to help you see your agreement with her and change it if you wish. Your clairvoyance can also help you see how she reflects you and what you need to change in yourself that you do not like. It is wise to take advantage of our opportunities so that we do not have to repeat the lesson with another person. It is also helpful to be clear about your agreements with the people you love. You learn the most from people with whom you have the greatest energy invested. You learn from loved ones as well as enemies, and both groups reflect you.

Two friends had a mutual friend who was having emotional difficulties. One friend used her clairvoyance to see her agreements with the woman in trouble, while the man got caught in his emotions and judged the struggling friend. The spiritually focused woman was a healing presence to both her friends. The man who would not acknowledge his agreements was a disturbance to the healing process. It is helpful to see our agreements and what we can learn from each other. When we allow ourselves to see clearly, we provide a spiritual perspective and are a healing presence.

Practice healing yourself by grounding and using your clairvoyance to see yourself and others clearly.

BE GROUNDED, and use your grounding to release any unwanted energy.

BE IN THE CENTER of your head. Look at a person whom you are using to learn about yourself. Let yourself see the lessons you are learning from this person.

CREATE A ROSE, and release any judgement about the lesson into the rose and explode it. Create and explode roses to release judgement until you can see from neutral.

LOOK AT YOUR EMOTIONS about the lesson. Create and explode roses to release emotional energy from the relationship. Allow yourself to see the interaction as a learning experience.

USE YOUR GROUNDING to release any resistance to the lesson. Take a few deep breaths and release resistance down your grounding cord.

BE IN THE CENTER OF YOUR HEAD and grounded, and accept yourself and the other person as you are. Release energy by creating and letting go of roses.

You can use all of your techniques to cleanse the energy from your system. Running your earth and cosmic energies will clear away emotional and other energies to help you learn your lesson.

You can also change agreements by using your techniques. Operate as spirit and the techniques can help you heal yourself.

BE GROUNDED and in the center of your head. From the neutral place in the center of your head, look at an agreement that you have which you no longer want. Create a rose, put the agreement into the rose and explode the rose, removing foreign energy from the agreement.

USE YOUR GROUNDING TO RELEASE emotional energy from your system. Allow yourself to be in the present with the agreement.

CREATE and let go of roses to clear ways you are like the other soul with whom you have the agreement. Do this until it is clear, whether you need the agreement any longer or not.

RUN YOUR EARTH and cosmic energies to cleanse energy from the agreement out of your system. Let the energy flow down your grounding cord.

CREATE AND LET GO OF ROSES to release judgement about the agreement. Create and explode roses for the agreement and let it go.

BE GROUNDED and in neutral, and allow your energies to run to readjust your system.

This exercise may take you several sessions to complete as we often have a great deal of energy tied up in agreements. By being neutral, you can let go of the agreement, if you wish to, by forgiving yourself and the other soul.

It is also helpful to look at agreements you like and cleanse them so they will remain clear and healing. By cleansing foreign energy from your agreements, you can create what you want instead of what someone else wants for you. For example, it is helpful to clear your mother-in-law's energy from your marriage agreement because she undoubtedly has different ideas about what your agreement should be than what you have.

By using your clairvoyance you can heal any aspect of your life, from spiritual agreements to physical health.

When you turn within and develop your clarity and neutrality, you see what is, what you want to change and how to change it. Clairvoyance helps you avoid the stumbling blocks you so often fall over when you are working in the dark without your clear seeing.

Each of us has an agreement with our body. We need to be in the present with this agreement and take responsibility for our body.

GROUND, be in the center of your head and look at something about your body you want to heal.

CREATE A ROSE, and release any interference to healing your body into the rose and explode it. Create and explode several roses for this interference. Run your earth and cosmic energies, and allow the flow of energies to wash away what you need to clear. Let the energy flow down your grounding cord.

FOCUS IN NEUTRAL, in the center of your head, and see the spiritual lesson of this healing project. Allow time to use your techniques to own and learn this lesson.

GROUND, CENTER, run your energies and create and explode roses to heal this physical imbalance.

You need to allow time to heal yourself. Use your clairvoyance to see the project clearly and to see how to heal it. Focus on the healing project in your meditations until you complete it. It can take anywhere from one session to several years of attention, depending on the intensity of the project and the amount of energy you have invested in it. Your clairvoyance will allow you to see what is and what to do.

Open your clairvoyance, and you begin not only to see yourself but to see others. This is when you need to realize that you are responsible only for your personal creativity. Every soul is responsible for what he or she creates in the body. We are not responsible for the creativity of others. So when you begin to see aspects in other souls that you believe need healing, remember that it is their responsibility to heal them and not yours.

If you become too responsible for others, you will eventually have to turn your clairvoyance down or off. You will not be able to deal with the immense weight of the responsibility. You can communicate as you wish about what you see, but if you take responsibility for it all, you will be trying to play God and will find the part impossible for you to fill.

Since most of us were taught from birth to be responsible for others, this is a difficult lesson to learn. But it is a necessary one to learn in order to combine our clairvoyance and healing skills. If we are so responsible for others that we grieve over all the ills we see, we will soon be sick ourselves.

When we allow each soul the power of his personal creativity, we do not feel responsible for his experience and can be of assistance by responding to him. When we see clearly, as spirit, we heal and allow ourselves to be responsive to instead of responsible for others. We can find joy and lightness in our spiritual abilities.

We are all like children and need the time and space to learn. If we wait for the child to take her steps toward us, she creates her experience and has her personal power. We can be waiting to catch her, to cheer her on and to rejoice over her accomplishment, but we cannot take the step for her. Nor can we experience for her the necessary falls and difficulties in learning to walk. By responding to the child and her needs, we encourage and heal. If we try to walk for her, she never learns to walk, and we become frustrated and unhappy.

Just remember the child learning to walk when you are tempted to take responsibility for another soul. Ask yourself whether you are assisting or interfering. Are you encouraging or defeating? When you take responsibility for others, you invalidate them by indicating you do not believe they can do it for themselves.

If you respond, you encourage the other person to heal herself. Your clairvoyance will help you to see when you are being responsive or responsible in your healing. A simple thing to remember is to be responsible for yourself and responsive to others. Clairvoyance helps you see yourself and others clearly while you develop yourself as a healing presence.

CLAIRVOYANT READING

Everyone is clairvoyant. Clairvoyance means clear seeing. While most people have not developed this ability, some people have put their attention on their clairvoyant skills and become "readers." Clairvoyant readers often assist others who have not developed their clairvoyance. Clairvoyant readers are ideally healers focused on spiritual validation. However, some may use their clairvoyance for other purposes.

A reading done by a clairvoyant is a soul reading. It is a clairvoyant perception of a soul's creations. We are spirit and create our personal reality. As creators, we retain our experiences as memory to enhance our growth, just as a child remembers how to walk, talk and function in a body. We retain these memories from one body to another to enhance our continued spiritual growth through many lifetimes. We store our experiences in various forms of energy, such as mental image pictures, symbols and vibrations that can be seen by a clairvoyant. Clairvoyant reading is much like reading a book, as each of us is a spiritual "book" of experiences and lessons learned. Our "book" contains our experiences through all our lives, the things we have accomplished and the goals we have yet to achieve.

Clairvoyants are called readers because they are reading you like a book and telling you what they see. Words in a book are symbols that have meaning to one who can read words. The pictures, symbols, formulas and vibrations in your energy system are symbols with meaning to one who knows how to interpret them. The clairvoyant reads what you have written as spirit. This information that he or she reads and interprets for you can help you perceive yourself more clearly as a soul who is creating in this physical reality. A clairvoyant reading can provide spiritual validation and insight into your creative patterns.

An example of how a reader can help you is by reading your aura, pictures and symbols to bring light to an interaction between you and someone else. The reader may see a symbol in the fourth layer of your aura that is an agreement between you and the soul that is your father. This symbol, located in the layer of the aura that relates to affinity, could help you see a past life when this other soul was a friend. If you watched this friend be hurt in a past life and felt responsible for him, it would cause confusion in this life. Until you cleared the emotions around the past life experience, you would continue to feel guilty and responsible. This could cause you to feel guilty toward your father for no apparent reason in the present.

A reader can help you see interference to your growth and other problems from your present life, as well as validating your bright spiritual light. You can then clear these issues from your spiritual system and not have to create through them any longer. You can also train yourself to see these things and use your clairvoyance to heal yourself. You may see that the problems you are experiencing with a present relationship are problems brought forward from a previous relationship. For example, you could be trying to relate to your wife the way you related to your mother. Once you see this, you can let go of the past way of operating and allow the present relationship to be healed.

One woman who received a clairvoyant reading changed her life completely based on that one experience of being seen clearly. She had been in an abusive marriage for twenty-some years. Until someone else saw what she saw, it was difficult for her to feel strong enough to leave what she had, to create what she wanted. When someone validated her experience, she was able to leave the relationship and start a happy, productive life.

Another example of the power of a clairvoyant reading is a young woman who was confused about her life path and went to a reader for perspective. The young woman was validated about her healing abilities. She began to see herself as a healer, which changed her relationship with everything and everyone. She changed her work, her relationships and everything in her life as she focused on her ability to heal. She eventually became a spiritual healer. The clairvoyant reading helped her see herself as capable, powerful and full of light. She had been criticized and invalidated about her healing skills for so long that it took a neutral party to help her see her true self again.

Anyone can benefit from a psychic reading. A reading can provide clarity, neutrality and amusement about our creations in this life plus information from past lives that is affecting us in the present. The main benefit of a reading is the validation or acknowledgement of ourselves as spirit. It confirms that all things are seen and known. There is a natural hunger for the validation of being a part of all that is, and a reading helps us to remember our spiritual self and abilities. The spiritual communication during a reading is the most exciting aspect of a reading since we experience ourselves and another person as spirit during the interaction.

A clairvoyant reading can be a wonderful, exciting experience because the reader sees you and validates who you are and what you have created. There is the experience of being known intimately by a person you may never have met before. Often people make the comment about how much a reader sees about them without knowing them. This ability to read our aura, pictures and other identifying spiritual symbology truly validates our spiritual nature. A reading allows communication on a spiritual level, which is a new and exciting experience for many people.

While some people are frightened about the lack of privacy afforded by the use of clairvoyance, the compensation is the elimination of loneliness. It takes time to accept as much openness as the use of our clairvoyance allows. It also requires a commitment to clear the many physical limits by which we define our lives. It is worth the challenge to experience spiritual awareness and communication on the level we are all capable of doing. We have the ability to see ourselves and others as spirit. This enables us to be accepting and forgiving about everyone's life experiences. All it takes is the desire to reawaken our clairvoyance and the perseverance to move through the interference to having clear spiritual sight.

Sometimes there is confusion about clairvoyance when one goes to different clairvoyant readers and comes away with different information. Some people then invalidate the process. The reality is that both readers could have given accurate information but from a different vibration. The person receiving the information needs to evaluate the information and accept what is correct for her from any reader. She needs to be responsible for herself.

Another thing that can confuse people about a clairvoyant reading is the fact that not everyone will allow himself to be read. A reader opens herself to the one being read and becomes vulnerable in the process. Sometimes the readee is belligerent or wants to play "prove it to me" games, instead of being validated as spirit. This can be damaging to the reader and can make the reading impossible. Some people cannot be read because they are so angry or filled with hate that the reader finds it difficult or even painful to open to them.

A clairvoyant reader, whether a professional or one who is developing clairvoyance for self-healing, provides an opening to the spiritual realm. This opening allows everyone involved a new awareness of himself as spirit and his relationship with God. The spiritual perspective you can gain from a reading, whether from yourself or someone else, can help you to have greater control over your creations. Using clairvoyance can help you get the spiritual assurance you need to lighten the load of daily life.

For example, if you are angry with someone, your clairvoyance may help you see that you are actually angry with yourself. You may have allowed someone else to use you or abuse you in some way, and you are angry for being vulnerable or weak. It could stem from a past life association that you have not completed. As you gain your spiritual perspective, you can forgive both the past and present, allowing yourself to complete the lesson. This clear sight can help you heal and become strong.

You need to be aware that you see the world through your perception of life. You view life through your own concepts, ideas and beliefs. This is true for all of us, including professional clairvoyant readers. The clarity and neutrality of the reader create the clarity of the reading. In other words, if the reader has healed himself, the reading will be healing. However, you can receive clear information from an unclear reader if you take responsibility for yourself and listen carefully to what is true for you and what is not. A reader may have a way of reading that does not appeal to you but may give information that is beneficial. It is up to you to listen and accept what is worthwhile for you.

Since you see reality through your own beliefs, it is important to avoid giving advice or accepting advice when using clairvoyance. A reader may see you clearly, but only you know what is correct for you to do with the information. It takes discipline to stop yourself from giving advice or accepting it, even when you know it is not correct.

When someone gives advice to another, he is really giving it to himself. In some way, the other person has reminded him of himself, and he is actually talking to himself. If we use our clairvoyance simply to communicate, rather than to influence, everyone is allowed their personal freedom. This requires that we all take responsibility for ourselves and our personal life lessons instead of trying to take responsibility for others.

When we begin to read others, we need to keep in mind that we must develop the ability to read ourselves. We can only give to others what we have within ourselves. So if you are not neutral or clear about yourself, how can you pretend to provide this for others? All of us can read each other's "pictures" or life creations, but are we able to do this from neutral, without judgement or punishment of the readee?

Clairvoyant reading provides us with information about ourselves as spirit and about how we are creating in the physical world. It gives us validation, assurance, information and spiritual awareness. Whether you are reading yourself, someone else or having someone read you, the experience opens you to your communication with the spiritual realm. By learning to read spiritually, you will eventually be able to use your sight to help you experience your relationship with God within.

Neutrality

B y using your clairvoyance, you develop your neutrality. Neutrality is balanced because it is neither positive nor negative. Neutrality does not take sides. Neutrality, from a spiritual perspective, is the ability to be non-judgemental. It is the ability to see what is and not what we or others wish us to see.

Neutrality is experienced best within the body from the sixth chakra, which is located at the brow. Neutrality is both a place in one's energy system and a state of being. We train ourselves to be neutral by clearing from our system the concepts that cause us to judge. We develop neutrality by focusing our attention in the sixth chakra to open and develop our clairvoyance. We are spirit and can be anywhere. We can leave our physical body, as we do when sleeping or sometimes in meditation. We can be in our body, and the place to be in the body to be neutral is the center of the head. Any other location in the body, except the top of the head, can pull you into the body levels such as the emotions.

Opening and using our clairvoyance can be both exciting and frightening since we usually begin to see both the beautiful and the ugly, the good and bad, within all things. When we operate as spirit and use our spiritual skills, we see the entire spectrum, not just what we want to see. This full view frightens some people, so they turn down their abilities in order to protect themselves from seeing the existing reality. Many people have experienced seeing a future event that was frightening or communicating with a soul who died. These experiences may have been so disturbing that the person turned down their clairvoyance to stop having these upsetting experiences. It only turns off the awareness of the encounters. Turning down one's abilities does not protect anyone. It is like an ostrich sticking its head in the sand with the remainder of its body still exposed.

The physical circumstances that cause one to diminish his or her spiritual skills can be identified and overcome by using the spiritual techniques to gain mastery of the body. Some body phenomena interrupt neutrality and need to be faced during the healing process. We can learn to work with the body rather than being controlled by it.

Fear is one cause of a great deal of static in our neutrality. When there is fear, the body seeks to be in control in order to protect itself and feel safe. When the body is in control, vibrations emerge that spirit does not enjoy. Spirit will often leave the body to its own devices when the body is filled with these energies. We, as spirit, do not like to be in a sea of pain, fear, hate or other debilitating energies, so we leave our body on its own when these energies dominate.

It is helpful to remember that we either create or accept all of the things we have stored within our body and therefore are responsible for them. When we do not take responsibility for our creations, we get into the habit of leaving the body in charge and in difficulty. We forget that we can clear the debilitating energies such as fear and pain. In fact, we can clear these creations much more easily than we produced them.

One of the things we need to do, as spirit, is to train ourselves to stay with our body when it needs us, instead of leaving it. Our spiritual techniques help us to focus on our body and learn to work with and through it. We can retrain ourselves as spirit to use our body effectively as a vehicle for communication and creativity. It is also necessary to retrain the body to accept us, as spirit, and our spiritual purpose in this world. The body must learn to allow us to abide in the center of its head.

To fulfill our spiritual purpose, we need to heal ourselves, including our relationship with our bodies. Our neutrality is necessary for the healing process and a result of healing ourselves, so developing neutrality is a process.

When we can see each creation as a spiritual experience, we can let it go or forgive ourselves. Forgiveness is necessary so we will not hold on to the experience or the emotions about it. When we become neutral about our creative learning process, we accept ourselves as we are and can grow and change. This way we mature and achieve our spiritual goals.

For example, you may have a pain in your finger that you cannot explain physically. You may remember that your younger brother hit that finger with a hammer when you were children and you have not forgiven him for that. If you look at the experience physically, you may only see a pain in your finger, or, at best, you will see anger and conflict. If you look at the experience spiritually with your clairvoyance, you may see an interaction that gives you insight into your relationship with this other soul. You can develop the neutrality to see that you were trying to get your brother to do what you wanted and succeeding, since you were larger. Your younger brother finally used violence to let you know that he objected to what you were doing. With a fuller view, you may find forgiveness for your brother and for yourself. You may even discover amusement about your childhood power struggles.

Neutrality provides a clearer and fuller view of life. When we view reality from any other perspective, we take the chance of allowing the physical perspective to overwhelm us. When we move out of the body to view this reality, we take the chance of losing touch with physical experience. Since we are creating in a body in the physical world, it is necessary to be aware of how things work here. We have to clear concepts which inhibit us, while simultaneously accepting the body reality we have chosen to work with and through.

For example, if you are in a female body, you have a vibration, lessons and circumstances which are particular to your female body. You selected a female body to learn certain things about yourself as spirit which could not be learned in a male body. This is also true for those who have chosen a male body. When you understand and embrace the gender characteristics you have created to learn through, your neutrality, understanding and power increase. You need to learn to work with your physical circumstances and not against them. Your neutrality helps you to do this.

Neutrality does not include judgement. It is a space from which we allow ourselves and others to be as we are. This does not mean we agree with everything; we simply allow it to be as it is. From this perspective, we learn a great deal about ourselves. We learn where we do judge and criticize. We learn our blind spots and weaknesses. Many do not want to develop neutrality because its development demands that we look at ourselves. When we can be neutral about self, we can be neutral about others.

If you are angry with someone, are you able to look from neutral at both sides of the picture? Can you see that you may be angry with yourself for some interaction and are projecting it onto the other person, possibly because of your fear or insecurity? Of course, anger at someone can be caused by her invading your space, but are you not more angry with yourself for allowing it to happen or to continue? Self-acceptance is a key part of the development of neutrality. To be truly neutral, you must be neutral about yourself.

Neutrality can assist in many situations. For example, you might see that your mother engulfed you when you were a child and you were not given permission to be yourself. As an adult, you would then expect the same behavior from other close female friends since you would equate love with being invaded. Since your relationship with your mother affects your relationship with all the women in your life, this pattern would require neutrality for you to change it. You might eventually see that your relationship with your mother is a lesson about how you relate to the planet. You might have been allowing the physical world to engulf you for many lifetimes and are ready to get back in touch with yourself as spirit. The invasive relationship could be a learning situation to help you realize that you can manipulate your personal life instead of being manipulated by physical circumstances such as an overly protective mother.

When you first see this sort of creation in your life, you experience anger, sadness and other emotional responses. If you continue to work with the experience from a neutral perspective, you get through the emotionality and begin to see the spiritual lesson. You cannot skip this step of healing emotionally. If you avoid the emotions, they will eventually resurface in some form. Once you gain your spiritual perspective, you find forgiveness for your mother and yourself. You can see that you are each playing a part to learn a spiritual lesson. If you have made mistakes during the learning process, you will also find forgiveness for these if you continue to use your clairvoyance and neutrality.

A friend of mine was so severely abused by her mother that she wanted to completely disassociate herself from her mother. My friend went through years of spiritual work and counseling to gain enough neutrality and forgiveness to associate with her mother again. Through her personal journey of forgiving her mother, she learned a great deal about herself. She learned how strong she is and also how much love she has to give. She discovered the love available to her from her husband, children and friends. She used her spiritual abilities and personal strength to create a new relationship with her mother and her world. My friend was angry, hurt and distant as long as she was not in neutral. She focused on being neutral about her past, and she gained control of her present.

Another friend is an amazingly powerful man who has recently discovered his spiritual nature. He is a capable clairvoyant and very neutral. His challenge is to validate his abilities and trust that other people want to hear his neutral spiritual perspective of life. His need to validate himself causes him to resist information from others, because most of the past information has been criticism or some form of invalidation. It is exciting to watch this loving, forgiving soul blossom as he learns to validate his neutrality and how he heals with his spiritual perspective.

Neutrality is a wonderful aspect of clairvoyance. Neutrality helps us be forgiving and accepting. The realization that God accepts and loves us as we are and does forgive all of our mistakes is a welcome discovery. We only need to learn how to forgive ourselves. The word "sin" is translated from Greek as "mistake," as if we were trying to do well but missed our goal. Sin can also be interpreted as missing the mark. We have traditionally misinterpreted the concept of sin and used it to control ourselves and each other with fear and guilt. We have used it to indicate that there is something basically wrong with us which may not be forgiven. We can more clearly understand what "sin" means from the spiritual perspective. From neutral, we see that sin is simply a challenge we have to overcome; a block we have placed in our spiritual path to rise above; a target we have missed. Like an athlete, we have to learn to jump the hurdles we create for ourselves. We have to learn to hit the mark, and if we miss it, to try again.

When we view sins as lessons to be learned, we free ourselves from judgement and the debilitating emotions that accompany the fear of being "bad." The fear, guilt and shame we experience from believing that something is wrong with us keep us from accomplishing our goals and rejoicing in life. With our clairvoyance, we can see the lesson and learn it, instead of falling into the trap of believing that we are innately evil because we had something to learn. Our neutrality develops as we practice seeing everything as a potential lesson.

It is unfortunate that so many institutions have become perpetrators of misconceptions about sin. Some religions teach children that they have done something wrong or sinned if they make any mistake. Since our learning process requires that we make mistakes, this causes a great deal of unnecessary emotional trauma. When a child is afraid that she has done wrong because she fell and hurt herself, we are reminded that we need to concentrate on clearing fear and guilt and bringing neutrality back into our lives. When a child can view life as an exciting learning experience, she can learn from any lesson. For example, she could learn from a fall that she simply needed to slow the body and practice coordination. If she is busy looking for her "sins" or "misconduct in the eyes of God," she will not learn anything except fear and doubt. We can undo the harm by clearing the guilt from ourselves and returning joy to our life lessons. We can teach our children and ourselves to see life as a joyous learning opportunity.

When we learn to create through the body with neutrality and joy, we learn to manifest our spiritual goals. By using our clairvoyance, we can gain a broader, clearer and more compassionate view of life. All of reality takes on a new promise and excitement when we see that every experience is an opportunity to learn and grow. Fortunately, God is never petty, as we sometimes are, and God created the master plan including learning, growth and forgiveness.

As spirit, we create our experience in this physical realm from our beliefs. We may have adopted these beliefs from our parents, siblings, peers, teachers or others during our developing years. We may also be operating from concepts we brought with us from past lives. This is the reason it is so important to clear beliefs that are not appropriate because the beliefs are the patterns through which we create our life. When we are taught that we are evil, sinful and guilty, and we believe this, we create our life through those beliefs. With our clairvoyance, we can develop our neutrality and clear our body and energy system of the unwanted beliefs. With our ability to see clearly, we can move out of fear and into joy.

The example of the child believing she was being punished by God because she fell shows how we get caught in destructive beliefs. She may have brought the belief from a past life or been taught the concept in school or church and accepted it. Either way, it is necessary for her to clear this belief so she does not have to go through life in guilt and fear.

Our neutrality is essential when deciding whether we wish to keep or discard a belief or concept. When we are neutral, we can see whether the idea is true for us or not. It could be true for someone else and a lie for us. In neutral, we can allow this difference and not have to judge the other person for having a different learning experience from ours.

For example, if your mother believed women must be subservient to men and you accepted this belief, you would be dealing with her concept in your life. This might be one of your mother's life lessons: learning to overcome subservience to others; or, possibly, she was an arrogant male in a past life and has to release energy from that incarnation. If you adopt this belief and use it as truth for yourself, it will disrupt your life. You will get off of your path with your lessons by trying to create through a belief which is a lie for you.

If you are female and try to be subservient when you are by nature a leader, it will confuse you and possibly cause you to get off of your life path. If you are male and adopt this belief from your mother, it could cause you difficulty with your relationships with women. You might be attracted to aggressive females and then try to make them comply with your adopted belief. This would confuse both of you.

When we see that life is composed of lessons to learn, it helps us to realize that each person must create life from his or her beliefs. When we try to operate through another soul's beliefs, we cannot learn our lessons. Our clairvoyance helps us see what is ours and what belongs to others, and our neutrality helps us forgive ourselves and others for the mistakes we make trying to live according to others' beliefs.

A view from neutral gives us the spiritual perspective to see ourselves and others as a part of God and not just as a body or part of the physical world only. When we broaden our view to encompass spiritual reality, our life takes on new meaning and joy. We see ourselves and others as powerful souls, creating our life experience to help us learn and grow.

Neutrality is sometimes identified with being cold and unfeeling. This is not true. Clairvoyance and neutrality do not stop us from feeling our emotions or having compassion. Our spiritual abilities allow us to be in control of our feelings and to rise above our emotions. The development of neutrality and clear seeing allows us to be less controlled by our bodies and more in control as spirit. A neutral perspective allows us to be clearer, more compassionate healers and helpers and more aware creators.

When our emotions are controlling us, we are not much help to anyone, including ourselves. The emotions are a communication from our body to us as spirit. Emotions are not the only way or even the most effective way to communicate with each other, although they do serve as effective attention-getters. When a loved one is in distress, we can assist him if we remain in neutral. When we become distressed along with him, we decrease our healing power and our ability to help him through his lesson.

Our clairvoyance helps us be neutral with ourselves and with the people about whom we feel the most emotion. The family is usually the group where we have our strongest emotional interaction. This is the group into which we chose to be born, so we are dependent on them for education, survival, support, emotional interaction, life lessons and more.

If we do not allow our neutrality about our family members, we can get overwhelmed with our emotions concerning them and lose our spiritual perspective. Since these are our closest physical relationships, it is a challenge to be neutral about this group and see them as spirit and not just as bodies. When we see the family members as spirit, it is easier to accept and love them as they are. Neutrality also helps us see what each member of the family has to give and to receive from the group.

Our neutrality does not make us cold or uncaring but helps us to be clear and accepting of each individual in the group. We all make mistakes as we thread our way through life. When we are neutral, we can forgive ourselves and the other members of the family for mistakes made. Our neutrality also helps us to be our unique selves within the group without being overwhelmed by the group. As we use our clear seeing and the neutrality it brings, we see what is ours and what belongs to each member of the group. Each person can then be set free to accomplish her personal goals instead of everyone trying to comply with the needs of one member of the group or focusing only on the survival of the group.

The most intimate physical relationship in this world is the one between mother and child. Our mother is the passageway through which we choose to enter the physical world. She is the soul we choose to house and nurture our body until it grows to the point where we can care for it. Our mother gives us a body and nurtures it with her body. She teaches us our most important life lessons.

You need your clairvoyance to be neutral about the soul that is your mother. Between conception and three years of age you learn a great deal from her about life in a body. You learn about giving and receiving, love and hate, male and female. You learn about your body and how to relate to it. It is important to learn to see your energy and hers as different. When you see the differences, you can allow her energy and beliefs to be hers and have yours for your creativity. Whether you love or hate your mother is inconsequential in your learning process. You need your clairvoyance to allow each of you to be the unique creative soul that you are. It is necessary to let go of her and for her to release you. You eventually need to let go of your dependence on your mother and learn to be an adult both physically and spiritually.

A friend of mine loved his mother a great deal. They were very close and had a wonderful relationship. His mother became sick, and he cared for her until she passed away. He was very disturbed during her illness, trying everything possible to heal her and keep her alive. One day, near the end of her life, while they were talking, she asked him to let her die. He was horrified because he could not imagine life without her. Fortunately, he came to me for help. Together we did healing work to assist him to let her go. He was able to rise above his emotions and gain neutrality about her need to leave her body and move on to her next life. He also accepted that he had the strength to go on and create a good life without this beloved soul in a body with him. Not long after his healing, his mother died. He was married within a year, and within two years, he and his wife had a daughter. They are both certain this soul is a reincarnation of my friend's mother, and I agree.

Being neutral is being spiritually focused. As spirit, we are not emotional or judgemental. The body communicates to us as spirit with emotions. We need to learn to control these emotions to create what we want and not allow the body to control us, as spirit. Attaining a state of neutrality about any aspect of life is a freeing experience. We are free from the ties of the emotions and the other limits of the body. We are free from other people's criticisms and praises. We are free because we see what is and are free to respond as we choose.

Being neutral does not eliminate our emotions or other aspects of our physical experience. It simply gives us our spiritual perspective and returns control to us, the soul. We are able to see the situation and relate maturely in a manner which is beneficial to all involved.

Neutrality gives us spiritual freedom. This freedom can bring great joy to anyone who wishes to have it. You must have a desire and a belief in the process and then give some time and attention for this freedom to develop.

Desire to be neutral, and believe that you can be, and it will happen. Practice the spiritual techniques and allow time to develop this ability to be neutral, and you will find it affecting every aspect of your life. Life seen from neutral is life with joy.

"With our spiritual sight, we can see that we create our life experience and can heal anything in our life. Clairvoyance allows us to see our lessons and how to learn them. It gives us the clarity to see our relationship with God."

Spiritual Perspective

Clairvoyance is a key to our spiritual perspective because it allows us to see spiritual phenomena. The spiritual world is always there and available for us to see. It is up to us to open our awareness to the spiritual realm and rise above the veil and limits of the physical world. This world is meant to be our creative paradise, but we often allow it to become our creative prison.

By opening our spiritual sight, we can begin again to see all that we are and all the ways we can communicate and create. We can see that we are spirit and a part of the Cosmic Consciousness. With our spiritual sight, we can see that we create our life experience and can heal anything in our life. Clairvoyance allows us to see our lessons and how to learn them. It gives us the clarity to see our relationship with God.

We are surrounded with an abundance of help from spiritual guides who wish to assist us with our journey. With our clairvoyance, we can see them and use their assistance. We can learn to tell the difference between beneficial spirits and those who are Earth-bound spirits who do not wish to help, but to manipulate.

Not all spirits without bodies are helpful. Your clairvoyance allows you to tell the difference. An easy way to decide whether a spirit is beneficial or not is to determine if it is invading your space. Your clairvoyance will tell you this. Any spirit who invades is not there to benefit. You must ask for help from the spirits who are here to help. They do not invade in any way.

When you open clairvoyantly, you can see your spirit guides, guardian angels and other spirits that are here to help you through your present growth. When you let yourself see, you are in charge of what is happening in your life because you relate to the spiritual realm as well as the physical one. You can easily determine who is beneficial and who is not. You can choose who you wish to relate to both spiritually and physically.

Your clairvoyance opens your awareness to the multitude of ways you communicate as spirit. You are not bound by the language of the body, either verbal, emotional, facial or otherwise physical. The language of spirit, which includes vibrations, mental image pictures, symbols, and formulas, is also available to you. The language of spirit includes all forms of communication and has the potential to flow like music.

As spirit, we project our state of being in the form of vibrations. We can use our clairvoyance to translate these vibrations into colors and then into words that the body can comprehend. Radio and television waves are an example of this in the physical world. We, as spirit, create pictures in which to store our information. We create symbols to show we have learned a particular spiritual lesson. These symbols are similar to Girl Scout badges because they indicate the accomplishment of certain lessons that a soul must learn. Formulas are like mathematical formulas. They carry a great deal of information in an abbreviated form and enable us to communicate on a higher level. As spirit, we use all these forms and levels of communication. If we are not conscious of communicating this way, we stay asleep to what is occurring within and around us.

Clairvoyance wakes us up to the multitude of spiritual communications within and around us. Our grounding and other spiritual techniques help us be in control of all of this spiritual communication. We can use our clairvoyance in every aspect of our life from the most mundane to the most sublime. It is available within each of us waiting to be awakened and used. By using this spiritual ability, we make our life and our world clearer and more loving.

By using your clairvoyance, you can see your relationship with another soul with much greater depth than by using only the body's language. With the body, you may determine your emotional and physical relationship. With your clairvoyance, you can see your spiritual agreements, your past life patterns, and incomplete cycles, what you have to learn from each other and much more. As you see pictures and symbols, you recognize how many similar ones you have with this other soul and how this brings you together.

When we see with our spiritual eyes, we see beyond the facades we have all created and see the soul as the soul is. Even if we have done things of which we are ashamed, we are still the bright beings who can forgive and clear the darkness. When we see, we become aware again that we can melt away the facades and let ourselves shine. With our clairvoyance, we can move beyond the judgement that usually holds us in the pattern of creating and maintaining facades.

If you allow yourself to be fooled by facades, you may find yourself in relationships and situations that are unpleasant and even detrimental to you. You may accept the facade someone gives you that he is a kind person and not heed the fear you feel when you are around him. You could find yourself in a dangerous situation by doing this.

By using your clairvoyance, you could see the person's intention to harm you because of a desire to punish anyone who is happy. There are souls who are not happy and do not wish to be happy and want everyone else to be miserable also. This is unfortunate but something we need to recognize as part of the free will nature of planet Earth. Not everyone wants to be healed, and each soul has the freedom to choose its path.

When you see, you are in charge of what you create and can keep the situation a healing one for you.

Using your clairvoyance can also help you find the souls you are meant to be with this lifetime. You will recognize them by their pictures, symbols, vibrations, formulas and other spiritual signs. This recognition assists you to maneuver through life with greater ease and joy. When you are with the souls you came to work with in a lifetime, you are happy.

Whether you identify with the more spiritually focused ideas of seeing pictures, symbols, auras, beings without bodies and other spiritual phenomena, or you simply wish to have a happier life, you can find your clairvoyance an asset.

With our clairvoyance, we can see that the great teachers of this world, such as Jesus, Buddha, Moses, Lao Tsu, Muhammad and many others, are here to assist us with our life decisions. These souls have developed themselves into enlightenment and are willing to help us do the same. By allowing ourselves to see the loving presence of these teachers in this world, we are encouraged and empowered.

The most important use of our clairvoyance is to see our relationship with God. When we see this clearly, we can change anything we need to in order to maintain our clear communication with God. Regardless of the many other ways we use our clairvoyance, we best use it to see our relationship with God.

The world is our place to learn and grow. The body is our creative communication tool. We are spirit. God is our source and goal. By using our clairvoyance, our path becomes clear. We see how to negotiate our way through life situations to accomplish our goals. We learn our lessons and mature, both spiritually and physically. Without our clairvoyance, we are like children groping in the dark. With our clairvoyance, we can be the joyous children of God we are meant to be.

The spiritual perspective that clairvoyance provides helps us make clear spiritual decisions. We are freed from creating only the body's desires or the wishes of another person. We are free to see things as they are and to be accepting and non-judgemental. Our clarity helps us avoid or step over the stumbling blocks so we have a clearer path in our relationship with God.

Clairvoyance, the conscious awareness of our spiritual perspective, frees us from the limits of the physical world. We see and it sets us free.

INDEX

Internationally known spiritual teacher, healer and clairvoyant reader **Mary Ellen Flora** is the author of twelve books & tapes, including her most recent, *Chakras: Key to Spiritual Opening* and *Meditation: Key to Spiritual Awakening*. Mary Ellen co-founded the CDM Psychic Institute and the Church of Divine Man, of which there are seven spiritual communities throughout the Western United States and Canada. She has devoted the past twenty-five years of her life to teaching thousands of people to meditate, heal and use their clairvoyance. Through her books, tapes and workshops, Mary Ellen reveals to each individual how to awaken spiritually and acknowledge their inner certainty. She currently resides in Washington with her husband and co-founder of the CDM Psychic Institute, M. F. Slusher.

If you wish to contact Mary Ellen or have her speak to your group, please contact CDM Publications at the following:

2402 Summit Avenue

Everett, WA 98201

Attn: Public Relations

(800) 360-6509

e-mail: cdmpub@c-d-m.org

Visit our website at www.c-d-m.org

CDM is a spiritual community and an international organization dedicated to spiritual freedom. If you are interested in learning more about CDM, or want information about the following topics, please contact the **Church of Divine Man/CDM Psychic Institute**.

- Clairvoyance
- Meditation
- Meditating with a group
- Healing
- Male & Female Energies
- Chakras
- Psychic Readings
- Kundalini
- Cosmic & Earth Energies

Church of Divine Man
CDM Psychic Institute

2402 Summit Avenue · Everett, WA 98201
Phone: (425) 258-1449 · Fax: (425) 259-5109
E-mail: cdm@c-d-m.org · Website www.c-d-m.org

Bellingham CDM
1311 "I" Street
Bellingham, WA 98225
(360) 671-4291
E-mail: bellingham@c-d-m.org

Seattle CDM
2007 NW 61st Street
Seattle, WA 98107
(206) 782-3617
E-mail: seattle@c-d-m.org

Portland CDM
3314 SW First Avenue
Portland, OR 97201
(503) 228-0740
E-mail: portland@c-d-m.org

Tacoma CDM
4604 N. 38th
Tacoma, WA 98407
(253) 759-7460
E-mail: tacoma@c-d-m.org

Spokane CDM
c/o 2402 Summit Avenue
Everett, WA 98201
(800) 360-6509
E-mail: spokane@c-d-m.org

Vancouver CDM
#201 - 1114 W. Broadway
Vancouver, BC V6H 1G5
(604) 730-8788
E-mail: vancouver@c-d-m.org

CDM Publications is a small press offering books and tapes of a spiritual nature. CDM Publications publishes guidebooks that give you information on how to meditate, balance your energy system and use your spiritual abilities.

Each publication offers easy-to-understand information on an aspect of spirituality and includes techniques to assist you in experiencing yourself, as spirit. Our books validate, inspire and offer insight and a new spiritual perspective.

CDM Publications
2402 Summit Avenue
Everett, WA 98201

Phone: (425) 259-9322
Toll Free: (800) 360-6509 · Fax: (425) 259-5109
E-mail: cdmpub@c-d-m.org
Website: www.c-d-m.org

If you have questions or are
interested in learning more
about clairvoyance, meditation,
healing, or other topics
concerning spiritual awareness,
please contact us.

CDM Publications 2402 Summit Avenue, Everett, WA 98201

Phone: (425) 259-9322 • Fax: (425) 259-5109 • Toll Free: 1-800-360-6509
E-mail: cdmpub@c-d-m.org • Website: www.cd-m.org

THE KEY SERIES BOOKS
by Mary Ellen Flora

		Quantity	Total
Meditation: *Key to Spiritual Awakening*	$10.00 US / $14.00 Canadian	_____	_____
Healing: *Key to Spiritual Balance*	$7.95 US / $11.00 Canadian	_____	_____
Clairvoyance: *Key to Spiritual Perspective*	$10.00 US / $14.00 Canadian	_____	_____
Chakras: *Key to Spiritual Opening*	$10.00 US / $14.00 Canadian	_____	_____

THE KEY SERIES AUDIO CASSETTES
by Mary Ellen Flora

Meditation: *Key to Spiritual Awakening*	$10.00 US / $14.00 Canadian	_____	_____
Healing: *Key to Spiritual Balance*	$9.95 US / $14.00 Canadian	_____	_____
Clairvoyance: *Key to Spiritual Perspective*	$10.00 US / $14.00 Canadian	_____	_____
Chakras: *Key to Spiritual Opening*	$10.00 US / $14.00 Canadian	_____	_____

THE ENERGY SERIES BOOKS
by Mary Ellen Flora

Cosmic Energy: *The Creative Power*	$12.00 US / $16.00 Canadian	_____	_____
Earth Energy: *The Spiritual Frontier*	$12.00 US / $16.00 Canadian	_____	_____
Male & Female Energies: *The Balancing Act*	$15.00 US / $21.00 Canadian	_____	_____
Kundalini Energy: *The Flame of Life* (Hardbound Edition)	$40.00 US / $50.00 Canadian	_____	_____

OTHER BOOKS AVAILABLE

I Believe: *Sermons* by M. F. "Doc" Slusher	$15.00 US / $21.00 Canadian	_____	_____
I Believe: *Sermons (Hardbound Edition)*	$30.00 US / $42.00 Canadian	_____	_____

SHIPPING & HANDLING:	
$4.00 first item, $1.00 each additional item. *Prices and availability subject to change without notice.* *No cash or COD.*	Sub-Total _____ Shipping & Handling _____ Tax (8.3% WA residents only) _____ **TOTAL** _____

☐ VISA ☐ MasterCard ☐ Call me for credit information - Phone _____

Card # _____ Exp. Date _____

Signature _____

Name _____

Address _____

City _____ State _____ Zip _____

E-mail Address _____